iPhone 15 for Seniors

A Comprehensive iPhone Guide for
Beginners with Step-by-Step Instructions

Darrell Goodman

Table of Contents

Introduction

In a world perpetually thirsting for innovation and seamless technology, Apple has been a wellspring of groundbreaking ideas, marrying design and functionality in a harmonious union. The unveiling of the iPhone 15 marks yet another illustrious chapter in Apple's storied journey, offering a glimpse into the future of mobile technology. Meticulously crafted, the iPhone 15 is not merely a communication device; it is a holistic experience, a multifaceted companion designed to elevate every aspect of our digital lives.

iPhone 15 amalgamates cutting-edge technology, unparalleled user experience, and a sleek, dynamic design, embodying Apple's ethos of continual evolution and commitment to excellence. This introduction aims to provide an initial exploration into the myriad features, innovative advancements, and potential societal impacts of the iPhone 15, setting the stage for a comprehensive examination of this revolutionary device.

Pinnacle of Innovation

Every aspect of the iPhone 15 is imbued with the spirit of innovation. From its crystal-clear display, rendering the digital world in vibrant hues and intricate details, to its advanced processing capabilities, ensuring a smooth, responsive interaction, the device exemplifies technological progress. It is a beacon of possibilities, inviting us to reimagine our relationship with technology and explore new frontiers in connectivity, productivity, and entertainment.

Elegance & Efficiency

True to Apple's design philosophy, the iPhone 15 seamlessly blends elegance with efficiency. Its refined aesthetics, characterized by sleek lines and a minimalist interface, are complemented by a suite of powerful features and applications, designed to cater to the diverse needs of the modern user. Whether capturing life's precious moments with enhanced camera technology or navigating the virtual realm with augmented reality, the iPhone 15 promises an immersive, intuitive experience.

Beyond the Device

The impact of the iPhone 15 extends beyond the confines of the device itself. It serves as a catalyst for change, fostering new ways of thinking and interacting in an increasingly digital world. The device's advanced capabilities have far-reaching implications for various sectors, including healthcare, education, and environmental sustainability, offering innovative solutions and paving the way for a more connected, harmonious future.

Chapter 1: Welcome to iPhone 15

1.1 What's New in iPhone 15

Breaking New Grounds

The unveiling of the iPhone 15 by Apple Inc. marks a significant leap in the world of smartphones, establishing new paradigms in technology, design, and user experience. This chapter delves into the groundbreaking features and enhancements that distinguish the iPhone 15, offering insights into the innovations that set it apart from its predecessors and competitors.

1. Revolutionary Display Technology

One of the first things users will notice about the iPhone 15 is its state-of-the-art display. Apple has introduced a new kind of screen technology that offers unrivaled color accuracy, brightness, and clarity. The adaptive refresh rate and improved touch sensitivity ensure a smooth and responsive user interaction, making every swipe and tap a joy.

2. Advanced Camera System

Photography enthusiasts are in for a treat with the iPhone 15's advanced camera system. Boasting enhanced sensors, innovative lens technology, and sophisticated image processing algorithms, the device promises stunning photo and video quality. New modes and features enable users to capture moments with unparalleled detail and creativity, bringing professional-grade photography to the palm of their hands.

3. Performance Boost

Under the hood, the iPhone 15 is equipped with a cutting-edge processor and optimized software, setting new standards in performance and efficiency. Whether navigating through apps, playing resource-intensive games, or multitasking, users will experience a level of smoothness and responsiveness previously unattainable in a smartphone.

4. AI and Machine Learning

The integration of advanced AI and machine learning capabilities makes the iPhone 15 smarter and more intuitive than ever. The device learns from user interactions, adapts to individual preferences, and offers personalized suggestions and features. This intelligence extends to various apps and services, enhancing user experience across the digital ecosystem.

5. Augmented Reality Experience

Augmented reality (AR) takes a front seat in the iPhone 15, offering immersive and interactive experiences. Users can explore digital elements integrated into the real world, play AR games, and utilize AR apps for education, design, and more. The advancements in AR technology open up new possibilities for entertainment, learning, and productivity.

6. Enhanced Battery Life and Charging

Addressing a crucial aspect of smartphone usage, the iPhone 15 features improvements in battery technology and energy efficiency. Users can enjoy longer usage times between charges, and the introduction of new charging technologies reduces the time required to replenish the battery, ensuring that the device is always ready when needed.

7. Sustainability Initiatives

Apple continues its commitment to environmental sustainability with the iPhone 15. The device incorporates eco-friendly materials, energy-efficient components, and a design focused on reducing waste. Users can enjoy cutting-edge technology while being assured that their device has been created with consideration for the planet.

8. iOS Advancements

The iPhone 15 is launched with the latest version of iOS 17, offering new features, enhanced security, and improved user interface. The advancements in iOS complement the hardware innovations, ensuring that users have access to a seamless and feature-rich experience.

Chapter 2: Getting Started

Embarking on Your Journey with iPhone 15

Congratulations on acquiring the revolutionary iPhone 15! As you unbox this masterpiece, you are not just unveiling a device; you're unlocking a gateway to a myriad of possibilities, innovations, and experiences. This chapter serves as your compass, guiding you through the initial steps of setting up and exploring the features that make iPhone 15 a technological marvel.

1. Unboxing and Initial Setup

- **Unveiling the Device**

As you lift the lid off the box, behold the sleek design and exquisite craftsmanship of the iPhone 15. Inside, you will find the device, a USB-C to USB-C cable, and documentation.

- **Powering On and Setup**

Power on the device by pressing and holding the side button. A welcome screen will greet you, prompting you to select your language and region. Follow the on-screen instructions to configure Wi-Fi, sign in with your Apple ID, or create a new one.

2. Personalizing Your Experience

- **Customizing Settings**

Dive into the 'Settings' app to customize your iPhone 15 according to your preferences. Adjust display brightness, set up wallpapers, configure notifications, and tailor privacy settings to ensure a secure and personalized user experience.

- **Arranging Apps and Widgets**

Arrange your apps and widgets to suit your usage patterns. The iPhone 15 allows for a highly customizable home screen, ensuring that your most-used apps are easily accessible. Explore the App Library for efficient app organization and access.

3. Exploring Advanced Features

- **Advanced Camera System**

Familiarize yourself with the advanced camera system of the iPhone 15. Explore various shooting modes, settings, and features to enhance your photography and videography experience. Experiment with Portrait mode, Night mode, and the innovative ProRAW format for professional-grade captures.

- **Augmented Reality (AR) Applications**

Dive into the world of augmented reality with the iPhone 15's AR apps. Explore AR games, educational apps, and interactive experiences that blend the digital and physical worlds, offering immersive and engaging content.

4. Connecting with the Apple Ecosystem

- **Syncing with iCloud**

Set up and sync your data with iCloud. iCloud ensures that your photos, documents, contacts, and other data are securely stored and accessible across all your Apple devices. Manage your storage plan according to your needs through the 'Settings' app.

- **Exploring the App Store**

Visit the App Store to explore and download a plethora of apps designed to optimize the capabilities of the iPhone 15. Discover apps across various categories such as productivity, entertainment, health, and more. Regularly update your apps to enjoy new features and enhancements.

- **Integrating with Other Apple Devices**

If you own other Apple devices, integrate them with your iPhone 15 for a seamless Apple ecosystem experience. Set up Handoff, AirDrop, and Continuity features to move effortlessly between your iPhone, iPad, Mac, Apple Watch, and AirPods.

5. Security and Privacy

Setting Up Face ID

Configure Face ID for secure and convenient access to your device. Follow the on-screen instructions to set up your data. These features also enable secure payments via Apple Pay and authentication for apps and services.

Managing Privacy Settings

Visit the 'Privacy' section in 'Settings' to manage app permissions, location services, and tracking preferences. Apple's commitment to privacy ensures that you have control over your data and how it is used.

2.1 Unboxing Your iPhone 15

Congratulations on unboxing your brand new iPhone 15! . This chapter will guide you through the cutting-edge features and functionalities that make the iPhone 15 a technological marvel.

So what did you get?

1. Retina XDR Display

Your iPhone 15 boasts the most advanced Retina XDR display ever seen on an iPhone. The high dynamic range and unparalleled resolution bring visuals to life with colors that are more vibrant and blacks that are truly black.

2. A16 Bionic Chip

Under the hood, the A16 Bionic Chip is the beating heart of your iPhone 15. This chipset offers remarkable energy efficiency and blazing fast speeds, ensuring a smooth and responsive experience, whether you're streaming, gaming, or using augmented reality applications.

3. iOS 17

The iPhone 15 runs on iOS 17, the most secure and efficient iOS to date. The user interface is not only intuitive but also  customizable, ensuring that your iPhone truly feels like your own. The revamped Control Center and Notification Center provide streamlined access and interaction with your apps and settings.

4. Camera System

The advanced camera system of the iPhone 15 is a photographer's dream. The Triple-Lens system offers unparalleled versatility,  allowing you to shoot in various modes ranging from ultra-wide to telephoto.

5. 5G Connectivity

With 5G connectivity, the iPhone 15 offers internet speeds like never before. Whether you're downloading movies, streaming  music, or playing online games, the lightning-fast connectivity ensures minimal lag and optimal performance.

6. MagSafe and Wireless Charging

The MagSafe feature allows for effortless attachment of a range of accessories, from wallets to chargers, while ensuring your  device is perfectly aligned for optimal wireless charging. With improved wireless charging speed, your iPhone 15 will be ready to go when you are.

7. Privacy and Security

Your iPhone 15 comes with enhanced privacy features, ensuring your data stays yours. The App Tracking Transparency feature allows you to have control over which apps can track your activity, and the new privacy dashboard provides a comprehensive overview of app data usage.

8. Health and Wellness

The Health app on iPhone 15 is more intelligent than ever, offering insights and recommendations to improve your wellbeing. The advanced sensors monitor your health metrics, including heart rate and sleep patterns, ensuring you stay informed and proactive about your health.

9. Sustainability

Apple's commitment to the environment is evident in the iPhone 15. The device is crafted using recycled materials, and the elimination of the power adapter and EarPods from the box is a step towards reducing carbon emissions. The Energy Star certification further attests to the energy efficiency of the device.

10. Exploring the App Store

With millions of apps available at your fingertips, the App Store is a gateway to endless possibilities. Whether you're into gaming, productivity, fitness, or photography, you'll find a plethora of apps designed to enhance your iPhone experience.

2.2 Anatomy of iPhone 15

1. Exterior Design

a) Front Panel:

- **Display:** The iPhone 15 boasts a ProMotion XDR display, offering vivid colors, sharp contrasts, and responsive touch interaction.

- **Notch:** The minimized notch houses advanced technology, including the Face ID sensor, front-facing camera, and speaker.

- **Edge-to-Edge Screen:** The expansive edge-to-edge screen maximizes your visual experience, allowing more immersive app interactions and media consumption.

b) Rear Panel:

- **Camera System:** The rear panel features a sophisticated camera system, including wide, ultra-wide, and telephoto lenses, accompanied by LiDAR and flash.

- **Apple Logo:** The iconic Apple logo sits elegantly in the center, symbolizing a legacy of innovation and quality.

- **Material & Finish:** The rear is crafted from Ceramic Shield and textured matte glass, ensuring durability and a premium feel. Titanium in the highest category of new products will replace stainless steel, which was prone to fingerprints.

c) Frame & Edges:

- **Material:** The aerospace-grade aluminum frame provides structural integrity while maintaining a lightweight feel.

- **Buttons & Controls:** The left edge houses the volume buttons and the alert slider, while the right edge features the side button and SIM card tray.

- **Ports:** The bottom edge includes: USB-C port **(2)**, microphone **(1)**, and stereo speaker. **(3)**

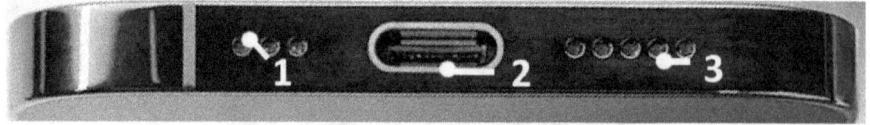

2.3 Turning On and Off

1. Turning On Your iPhone 15

- **Standard Power-On:** Press and hold the **Side button** located on the right edge of your device until the Apple logo appears on the screen. Release the button and wait for your iPhone to complete the startup process.

- **Setup Process:** The first time you turn on your iPhone, you'll be greeted with a series of setup steps. Follow the on-screen instructions to configure your device.

2. Turning Off Your iPhone 15

- **Standard Power-Off:** Simultaneously press and hold the Side button along with the Volume Up or Down button until two sliding buttons appear. Release the buttons and swipe the slider labeled "slide to power off" to the right.

- **Settings Option:** Go to Settings > General, scroll down to the bottom, and tap Shut Down. Slide to power off.

3. Restarting Your iPhone 15

- **Soft Restart:** Quickly press and release the Volume Up button, then the Volume Down button, followed by pressing and holding the Side button until the Apple logo appears. Release the Side button and allow the phone to restart.

- **Settings Restart:** There is no direct option to restart from the Settings menu. You need to power off the device from the Settings and then turn it back on using the Side button.

4. Emergency Shutdown & SOS

In critical situations, it's important to know how to shut down your device swiftly and call for help if needed.

- **Emergency Shutdown:** Perform the Soft Restart method but continue holding the Side button even after the Apple logo appears, until the device's screen turns black.

- **Emergency SOS:** Press and hold the Side button and one of the Volume buttons. Continue holding them as the countdown begins. After the countdown ends, your iPhone automatically calls emergency services.

2.4 Initial Setup

Now that you've unboxed your new device and are acquainted with its exterior brilliance, it's time to dive into the initial setup. This chapter will guide you through the essential steps to unleash the full potential of your shiny new gadget, ensuring a seamless and personalized user experience from the get-go.

1. Turning On Your Device

Start by pressing and holding the side button located on the right edge of your device. You'll be greeted by a welcoming 'Hello' in various languages, symbolizing the global unity and diversity embedded in every device. Swipe up to begin the setup process.

English ⟩

Español ⟩

简体中文 ⟩

繁體中文 ⟩

日本語 ⟩

Français ⟩

Deutsch ⟩

2. Selecting Your Language and Region

Choose your preferred language and your current region. These settings will affect how information is displayed on your device, ensuring a tailored experience from the onset.

3. Connecting to Wi-Fi

Connect your device to a Wi-Fi network by selecting the network and entering the password. A stable internet connection is essential for the setup, allowing your device to activate and download any necessary updates.

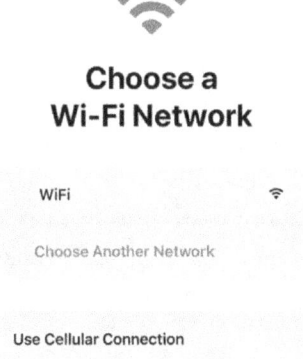

Choose a Wi-Fi Network

WiFi

Choose Another Network

4. Data Privacy and Protection

Use Cellular Connection

Your device will present information about Apple's data privacy policies. Take a moment to understand how your data is handled and protected, showcasing Apple's commitment to user privacy and security.

5. Setting Up Face ID Depending on your device model, set up Face ID. These features offer a secure and convenient way to unlock your device, make purchases, and log in to apps. Follow the on-screen instructions to capture your facial map or fingerprint.

6. Creating or Logging into Apple ID

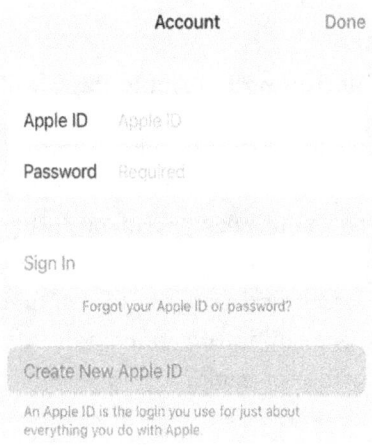

Account   Done

Your Apple ID is your gateway to the Apple ecosystem. If you have an existing Apple ID, log in with your credentials. If not, you will be guided through creating a new one. This ID will give you access to iCloud, App Store, iTunes, and more.

Apple ID   Apple ID

Password   Required

Sign In

Forgot your Apple ID or password?

Create New Apple ID

An Apple ID is the login you use for just about everything you do with Apple.

7. Restoring or Setting Up as New

You have the option to set up your device as new or restore from a previous backup. If you're a new Apple user, select "Set Up as New iPhone". If you're upgrading, choose to restore from iCloud Backup, iTunes Backup, **or transfer directly from another device.**

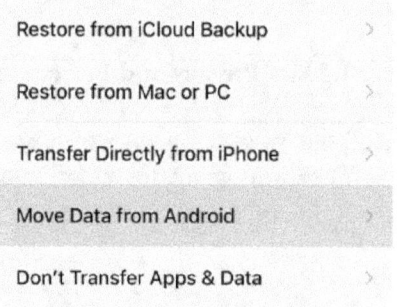

Apps & Data

Choose how you want to transfer apps and data to this iPhone.

Restore from iCloud Backup   >

Restore from Mac or PC   >

8. Agreeing to Terms and Conditions

Transfer Directly from iPhone   >

Move Data from Android   >

Review and agree to the Terms and Conditions. Take your time to read through the information to understand the user agreement you are entering.

Don't Transfer Apps & Data   >

9. Customizing Settings

During the setup, you'll be prompted to customize several settings, including Siri, App Analytics, and True Tone Display. Tailor these settings to suit your preferences, knowing you can always adjust them later in the Settings app.

 **Pay**

10. Setting Up Apple Pay

Add credit, debit, or store cards and use Apple Pay with Touch ID to make purchases easily and securely, right from your iPhone.

Add a credit or debit card to set up Apple Pay, allowing for secure and contactless payments using your device. Follow the on-screen instructions to capture your card information and verify with your bank.

Apple may use anonymous location data to improve its services. Your phone number, account, and location information may be sent to your card issuer to set up Apple Pay. About Apple Pay & Privacy...

Continue

11. Screen Time and App Downloads

Set up Screen Time to monitor and manage your device usage. Then, proceed to download essential apps from the App Store to enhance your user experience.

12. Finalizing the Setup

Finally, choose your preferred view (Standard or Zoomed) and finalize the setup. Your device will take a few moments to complete the configuration before welcoming you to the home screen.

2.5 Where to start?

1. The Home Screen Layout

Your home screen is the gateway to your device's myriad applications and features. Familiarize yourself with the layout, including the arrangement of app icons, the Dock at the bottom for your most-used apps, and the Notification Center that can be accessed by swiping down from the top.

2. App Library

Located to the right of your last home screen, the App Library automatically organizes all your apps into categories, offering a clutter-free view and making it easier to find the app you are looking for.

3. Control Center

Swipe down from the top-right corner to access the Control Center. Here, you can quickly adjust settings like brightness, volume, Wi-Fi, Bluetooth, and access a customizable array of quick function tiles.

4. Siri - Your Personal Assistant

Invoke Siri by saying "Hey Siri" or pressing and holding the side button. Siri can answer questions, send messages, play music, provide directions, and much more. The more you use Siri, the more personalized your experience becomes.

5. Gesture Navigation

Understand the various gestures for navigation, such as swiping up to go Home, swiping left or right to switch between open apps, and pinching with two fingers to zoom in or out.

6. Keyboard Shortcuts

Explore the in-built keyboard shortcuts for typing efficiency. Swipe typing, auto-correct, predictive text, and voice dictation are tools available to enhance your texting and emailing experience.

7. Settings App

The Settings app is the control room of your device. Dive into the various menus to personalize your device, adjust privacy settings, update software, manage storage, and much more.

8. App Store - Gateway to Applications

Discover the App Store, where millions of apps are available for download. Explore categories, top charts, and personalized recommendations to find apps that suit your needs and interests.

9. Camera and Photos App

Experiment with the Camera app and its various modes like Photo, Video, Portrait, and Panorama. After capturing memories, organize and edit them in the Photos app, where you can create albums, add filters, and adjust lighting.

10. Messages and FaceTime

Get acquainted with the Messages app for texting and the FaceTime app for video calls. Learn about the array of features available within these apps, including Memoji, stickers, effects, and group conversations.

11. Health and Wellness Features

Explore the Health app, which consolidates health and wellness data from your iPhone, Apple Watch, and third-party apps. Set up your Medical ID, input health data, and explore mindfulness and fitness features.

12. Emergency SOS

Familiarize yourself with the Emergency SOS feature, which allows you to quickly call emergency services by pressing and holding the side button and one of the volume buttons.

2.6 Apple ID and iCloud

1. Understanding Apple ID

Your Apple ID is the account you use to access all Apple services, including the App Store, Apple Music, iCloud, iMessage, FaceTime, and more. It consists of an email address and password, and it's safeguarded with security questions and two-factor authentication. It's the key that unlocks a seamless experience across all your Apple devices.

2. Creating an Apple ID

If you haven't created an Apple ID during the initial setup, you can create one by:

- Opening the Settings app.

- Tapping on "Sign in to your iPhone" at the top.

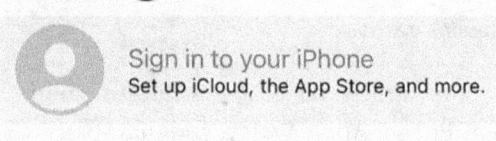

- Selecting "Don't have an Apple ID or forgot it?".

Apple ID

Sign in with your Apple ID to use iCloud,
iTunes, the App Store, and more.

Apple ID

Forgot password or don't have an Apple ID?

- Following the on-screen instructions.

3. Managing Your Apple ID

Once your Apple ID is active, manage your account details, security settings, payment information, and subscriptions through the Apple ID section in the Settings app. Regularly updating this information ensures uninterrupted access to Apple services.

4. Understanding iCloud

iCloud is a cloud storage and cloud computing service that lets you store photos, videos, documents, music, apps, and more, securely in the cloud. It seamlessly syncs this content across all your Apple devices, allowing for real-time access, anytime, anywhere.

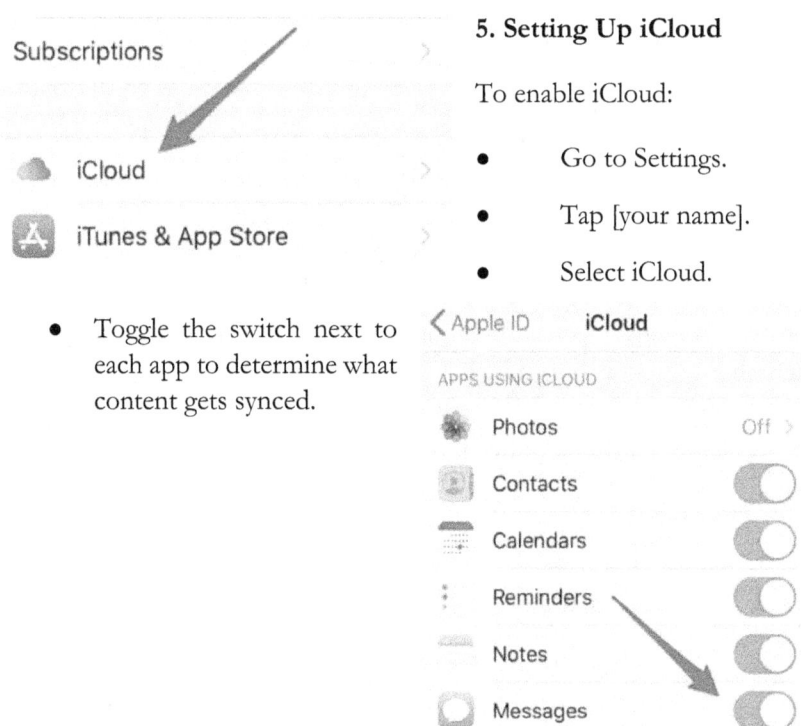

5. Setting Up iCloud

To enable iCloud:

- Go to Settings.

- Tap [your name].

- Select iCloud.

- Toggle the switch next to each app to determine what content gets synced.

6. iCloud Storage Plans

You get 5GB of iCloud storage for free. If you need more space, several upgrade options are available, ranging from 50GB to 2TB, which can be shared with your family. To change your storage plan, go to Settings > [your name] > iCloud > Manage Storage > Change Storage Plan.

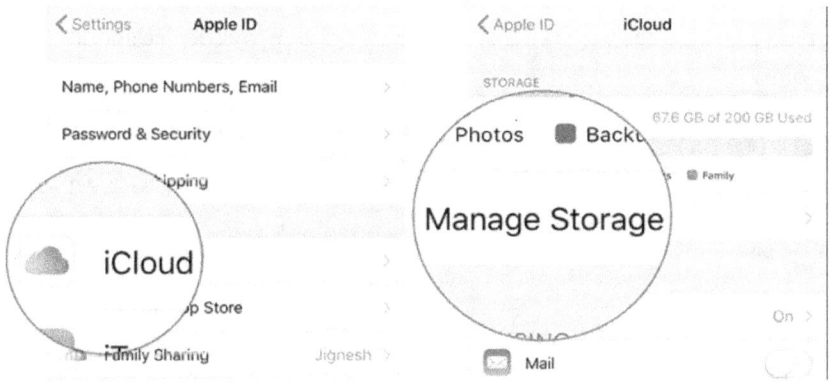

7. iCloud Backup

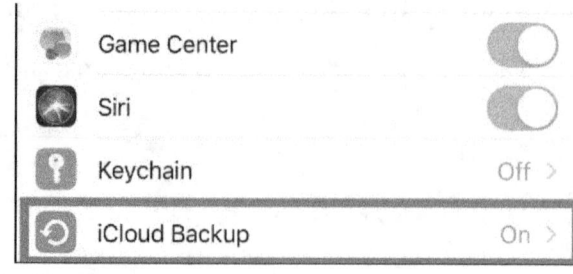

iCloud Backup automatically backs up your device's information daily over Wi-Fi. To ensure this feature is activated, navigate to Settings > [your name] > iCloud > iCloud Backup, and toggle the switch on.

8. Find My

The Find My app helps you locate your Apple devices, should you misplace them. Ensure that the Find My feature is enabled in Settings > [your name] > Find My. This feature is crucial for the security of your device and the data it holds.

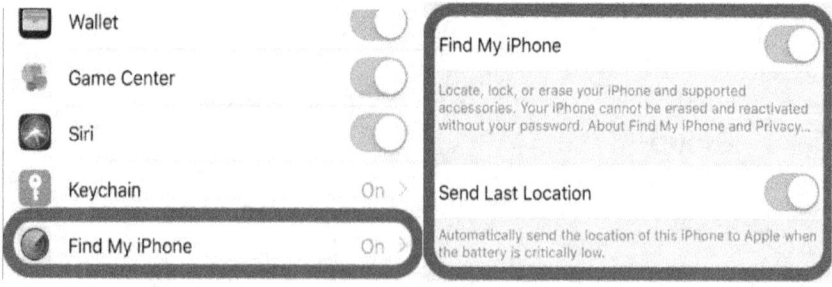

9. Family Sharing

Family Sharing allows you to share Apple purchases and subscriptions with up to five family members. It also lets you share photos, a family calendar, and more. To set up Family Sharing, go to Settings > [your name] > Family Sharing, and follow the on-screen instructions.

10. Sign Out and Deactivation

If you ever need to sign out of your Apple ID or deactivate it, navigate to Settings > [your name] > Sign Out. Remember, signing out of your Apple ID will disable iCloud and other Apple services on your device.

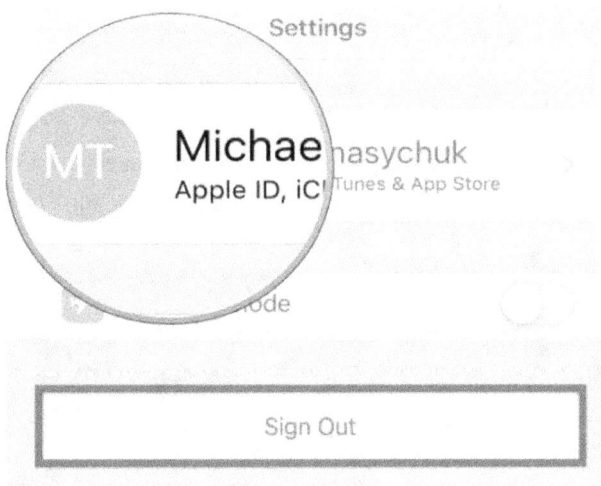

2.7 Using the Touch Screen and Gestures

1. Touch Screen Basics

a) Tap:

- The fundamental interaction – simply tap an app to open it, tap an option to select it, or tap a button to perform an action.

b) Swipe:

- Glide your finger vertically or horizontally across the screen to scroll through content, navigate between pages, or access additional options.

c) Pinch and Spread:

- Use two fingers to pinch or spread for zooming in and out on photos, maps, websites, and more.

d) Long Press:

- Holding your finger on an element for an extended period reveals additional options, contextual menus, or activates specific features such as moving apps.

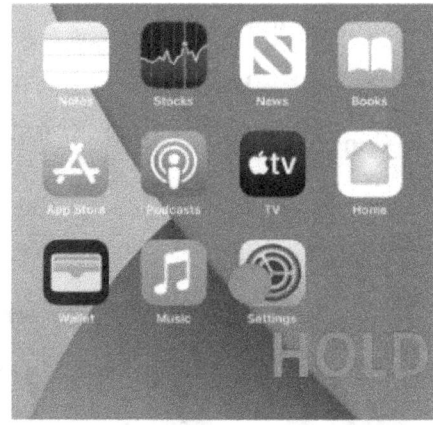

e) Drag:

- Touch and hold an item, then move it to a different location. Useful for rearranging apps, highlighting text, or adjusting sliders.

2. Gesture Navigation

a) Home Gesture:

- Swipe up from the bottom edge of the screen and release to return to the Home screen from any app.

b) App Switcher:

- Swipe up from the bottom edge and pause in the middle of the screen to view the App Switcher and quickly navigate between open apps.

c) Notification Center:

- Swipe down from the top-left corner or to access your notifications.

d) Control Center:

- Swipe down from the top-right corner to access the Control Center, where you can manage various settings and functions quickly.

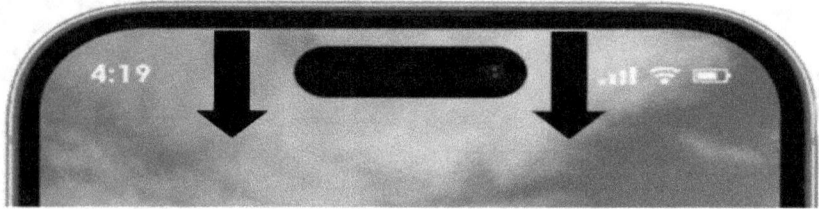

e) Quick App Switch:

- Swipe left or right along the bottom edge to switch between recently used apps swiftly.

3. Advanced Gestures

a) Siri Shortcuts:

- Customize and use gestures to activate Siri Shortcuts, which perform specific actions or automate multiple tasks at once.

b) Back Tap:

- Double or triple tap on the back of the iPhone to perform custom actions or shortcuts. Configure this feature in Settings > Accessibility > Touch > Back Tap.

c) Shake to Undo:

- Shake your device quickly to undo typing or an action and receive a prompt to confirm.

5. Cleaning and Caring for the Screen

- **Cleaning:** Use a soft, slightly damp, lint-free cloth to clean the screen. Avoid abrasive cloths, towels, paper towels, and avoid spraying cleaners directly onto the device.

- **Screen Protectors:** Consider applying a quality screen protector to safeguard against scratches and impact.

Chapter 3: Staying Connected

1. Cellular and Wi-Fi Connectivity

a) Managing Cellular Data:

- Navigate to Settings > Cellular to manage your cellular data settings, turn on/off mobile data, and adjust data usage for individual apps.

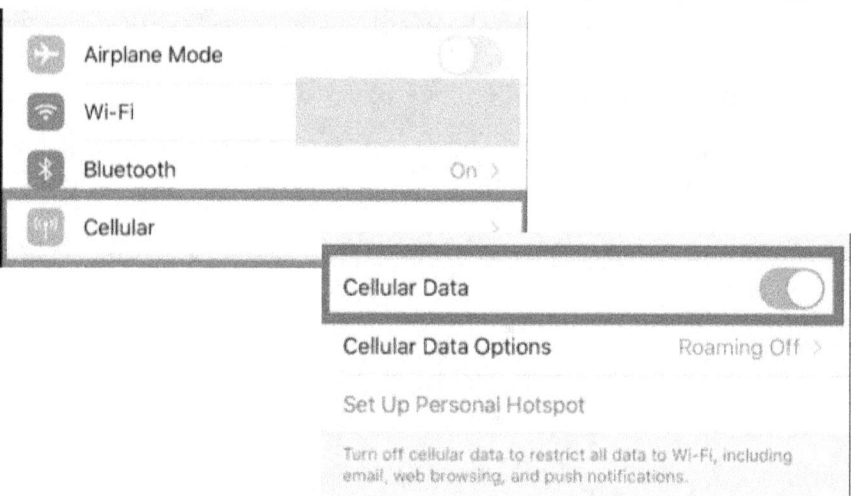

b) Connecting to Wi-Fi Networks:

- Access Wi-Fi settings under Settings > Wi-Fi to join networks, manage saved networks, and adjust related settings.

2. Making and Receiving Calls

a) Using the Phone App:

- Explore the Phone app's interface to make calls, access voicemail, view recent calls, and manage contacts.

b) Wi-Fi Calling and VoLTE:

- Enable Wi-Fi Calling and VoLTE (Voice over LTE) under Settings > Phone for improved call quality and connectivity.

- Make calls through applications such as WhatsApp, Skype, Facetime using an Internet connection.

3. Sending and Receiving Messages

a) iMessage and SMS:

- Utilize the Messages app to send text, photos, videos, and more to other iPhone users via iMessage or as SMS/MMS to non-iPhone users.

b) Message Effects and Features:

- Discover various message effects, stickers, and features like message pinning, inline replies, and mentions.

4. FaceTime for Video and Audio Calls

a) Making FaceTime Calls:

- Use the FaceTime app to make video and audio calls to other Apple devices.
- Explore Group FaceTime, SharePlay, and new audio and video effects.

b) FaceTime Links:

- Create and share FaceTime links to invite others to a FaceTime call, including non-Apple users.

5. E-Mail Communication

a) Setting Up Email Accounts:

- Navigate to Settings > Mail > Accounts to add and manage email accounts.

- Adjust mail settings such as preview lines, swipe options, and notifications.

b) Using the Mail App:

- Familiarize yourself with the Mail app's interface to compose, send, receive, and organize emails.

6. Using Social Media and Communication Apps

- Explore the App Store to download and install a variety of social media and communication apps like WhatsApp, Facebook, Instagram, Twitter, and more.

7. Browsing the Web with Safari

a) Exploring Safari Features:

- Use Safari to browse the web, bookmark pages, manage tabs, and explore new privacy features and customization options.

b) Safari Extensions:

- Discover and install Safari extensions from the App Store for additional functionalities and features while browsing.

8. Staying Informed with News and Podcasts Apps

- Utilize the News app to stay informed with the latest news from various sources and topics.

- Explore the Podcasts app to discover, subscribe to, and listen to a wide range of podcasts across different genres.

9. Using AirDrop and Nearby Share

- Enable and use AirDrop to share files, photos, and more with nearby Apple devices.

- Explore Nearby Share for sharing content with Android devices.

3.1 Making and Receiving Calls

1. Using the Phone App

a) Keypad and Contacts:

- Access the keypad for manual number entry and browse your contacts list for saved numbers.

- Tap on a contact to view multiple calling options, including voice calls and FaceTime.

b) Favorites and Recent Calls:

- Manage your favorite contacts for quick dialing and view your call log under the 'Recents' tab.

- Swipe left on a call log entry to reveal additional options such as blocking and reporting.

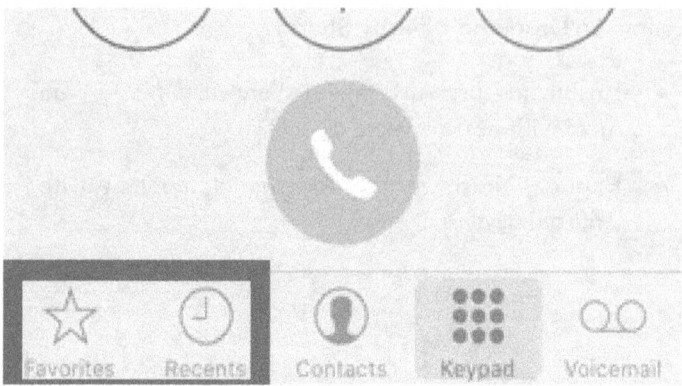

2. Receiving Calls

a) Answering and Declining:

- Swipe up to answer incoming calls or swipe down to decline. You can also use the side button to silence the ring.

- For FaceTime calls, two additional options appear: "Remind Me" and "Message."

b) Managing Notifications:

- Customize call notifications under Settings > Phone to adjust banners, sounds, and vibration settings.

3. During a Call

a) In-Call Options:

- Explore the in-call menu to access options like speaker, mute, and add call.

- Use the contacts button to add additional people to the call.

b) Recording Calls:

- Although iOS does not natively support call recording, third-party apps are available. Ensure compliance with local laws regarding recording consent.

4. Voicemail Setup and Management

a) Setting Up Voicemail:

- Open the Phone app and tap on the voicemail tab to set up your voicemail, including creating a password and recording a greeting.

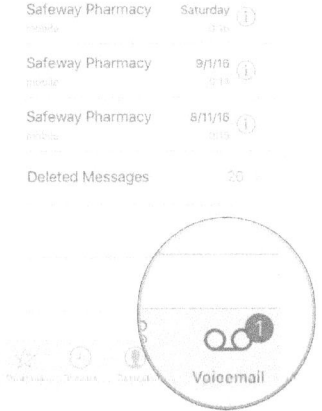

b) Visual Voicemail:

- Listen to and manage your voicemail messages directly from the voicemail tab with visual voicemail.

5. Call Forwarding and Blocking

a) Call Forwarding:

- Manage call forwarding under Settings > Phone > Call Forwarding to redirect incoming calls to another number.

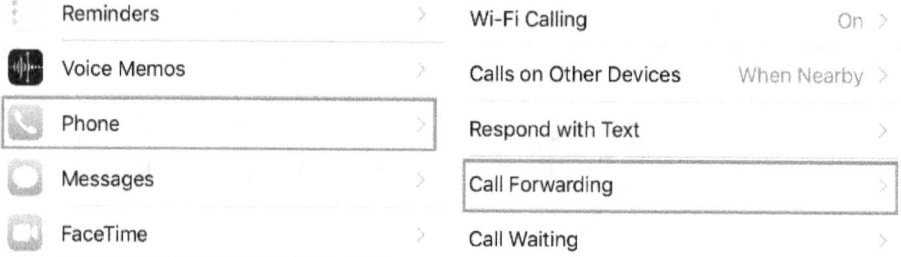

b) Blocking Numbers:

- Block specific contacts or unknown callers under Settings > Phone > Blocked Contacts.

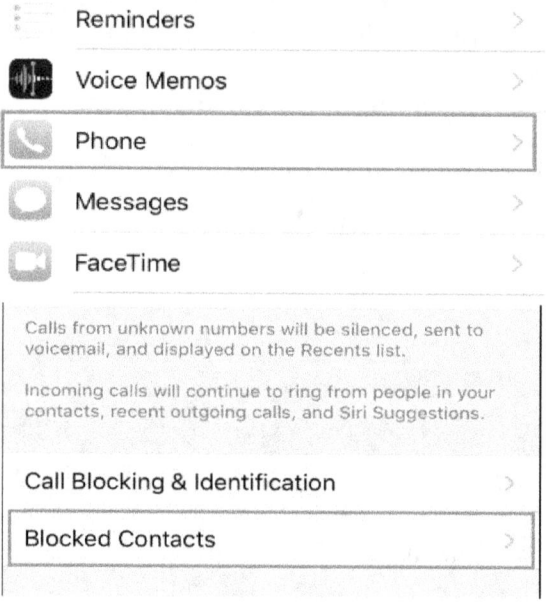

6. Wi-Fi Calling and VoLTE

a) Wi-Fi Calling:

- Enable Wi-Fi Calling under Settings > Phone to make and receive calls over Wi-Fi when cellular service is unavailable.

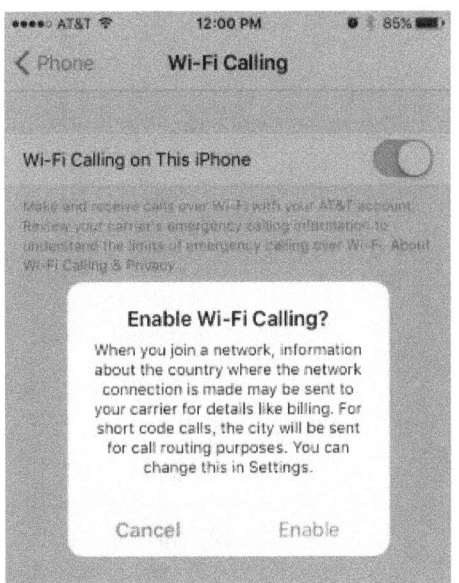

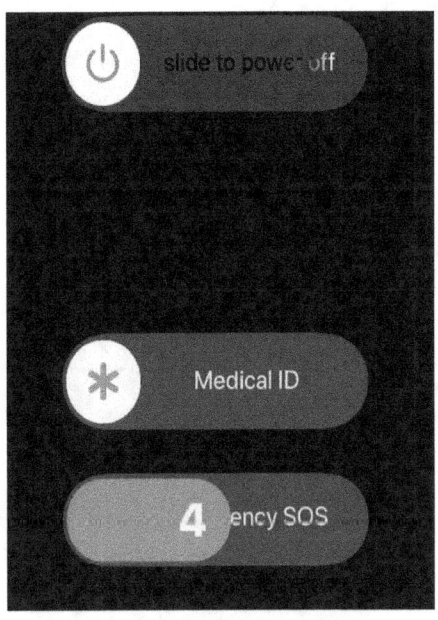

7. Emergency Calls

- press and hold the side button and one of the volume buttons for about two seconds until you see the Emergency SOS slider appear. Drag the slider to the right to call emergency services.

- Familiarize yourself with Emergency SOS and Medical ID for added safety.

3.2 Sending and Receiving Text Messages

1. The Messages App

a) Navigating the Interface:

- Familiarize yourself with the layout of the Messages app, including the conversations list, search bar, and the composition button.

- Learn how to start new conversations, manage group chats, and view message details.

b) iMessage and SMS/MMS:

- Understand the difference between iMessage (blue bubbles) and SMS/MMS (green bubbles).

- Enable or disable iMessage under Settings > Messages.

2. Composing and Sending Messages

a) Text Input and Keyboard:

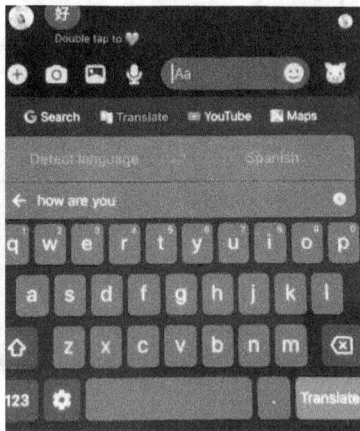

- To invoke the keyboard, click on the text input field.

- Explore keyboard settings, including text replacement, predictive text, and emoji.

b) Sending Media and Attachments:

- Learn how to send photos, videos, voice memos, and document attachments.

- Explore the app drawer for additional content, like GIFs, Apple Pay, and App Store integrations.

3. Managing Conversations

a) Pinning and Deleting:

- Keep important conversations at the top by pinning them.

- Swipe left on a conversation to delete or archive it.

b) Muting and Blocking:

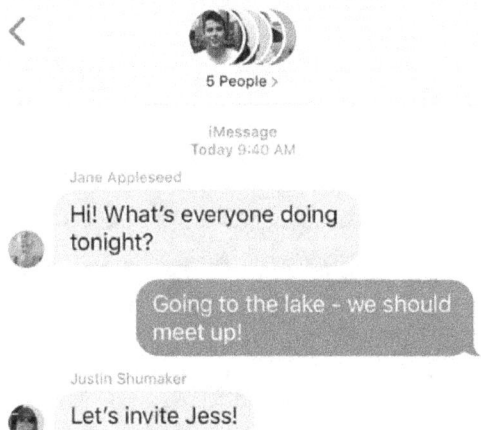

- Manage notifications by muting individual conversations or blocking contacts.

- Explore customization options for notifications under Settings > Messages.

4. Group Chats and Mentions

a) Creating and Naming Group Chats:

- Start group chats by adding multiple contacts and set a group name and photo.

- Learn how to add or remove participants and leave group chats.

b) Inline Replies and Mentions:

- Keep group chats organized with inline replies and mention individuals to notify them directly.

5. Audio Messages and Voice Dictation

a) Sending Audio Messages:

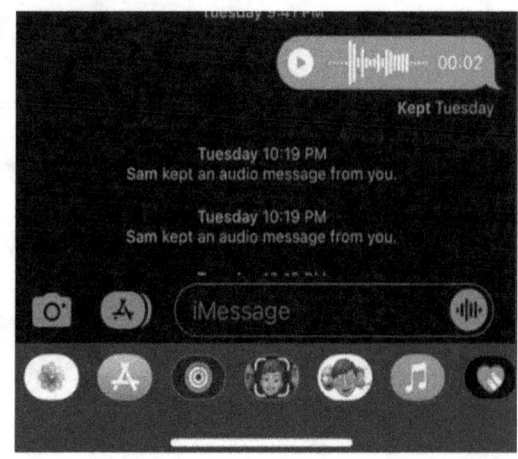

- Record and send audio messages by holding down the microphone icon.

- Adjust audio message settings under Settings > Messages.

b) Voice Dictation:

- Use voice dictation to compose messages by tapping the microphone on the keyboard.

6. Message Search and Archiving

a) Searching Messages:

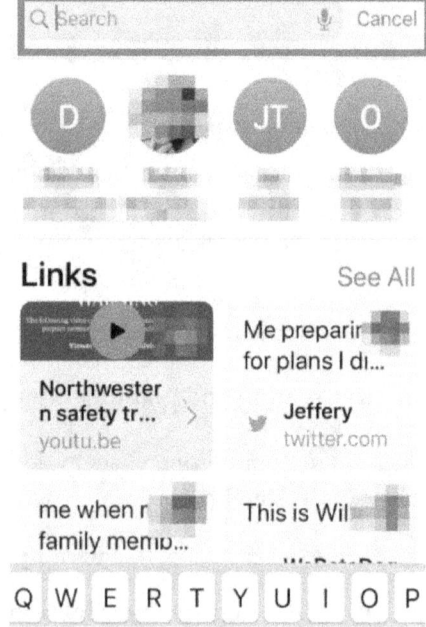

- Utilize the search bar to find specific messages, images, links, and attachments within conversations.

7. Privacy and Security

a) End-to-End Encryption:

- Understand how iMessage uses end-to-end encryption to secure your messages.

- Learn about SMS/MMS security considerations and how to identify phishing attempts.

b) Reporting and Filtering:

- Report spam or junk messages and enable filtering for unknown senders under Settings > Messages.

3.3 Setting Up Email Accounts

1. Adding Email Accounts

a) Supported Email Providers:

- Your iPhone 15 supports a variety of email providers, including iCloud, Google, Yahoo, Outlook, and more.

- For other providers, you might need to enter server settings manually.

b) Navigating to Account Settings:

- Open Settings and scroll down to "Mail."

- Tap on "Accounts" and then "Add Account" to begin the setup process.

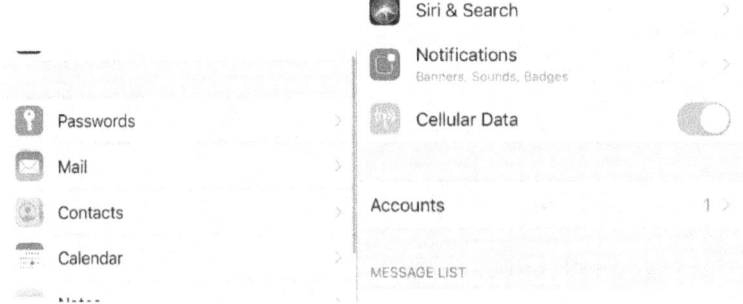

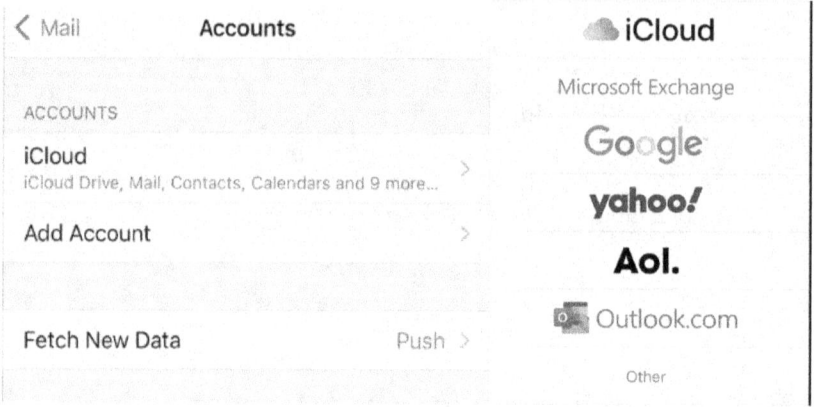

2. Inputting Account Information

a) Entering Email Address and Password:

- Select your email provider and enter your email address and password.

- Follow the on-screen prompts to authenticate and grant necessary permissions.

b) Manual Setup:

- If your email provider is not listed, select "Other" and choose "Add Mail Account."

- Enter your name, email address, password, and a description for the account.

- Input the incoming and outgoing mail server settings provided by your email provider.

3. Customizing Account Settings

a) Sync Settings and Notifications:

- Once added, tap on the email account to customize settings, such as mail syncing and notification preferences.

b) Fetch New Data:

- Under Settings > Mail > Accounts > Fetch New Data, set how often your iPhone will check for new emails.

- Choose between push, fetch, and manual options based on your preference and battery efficiency considerations.

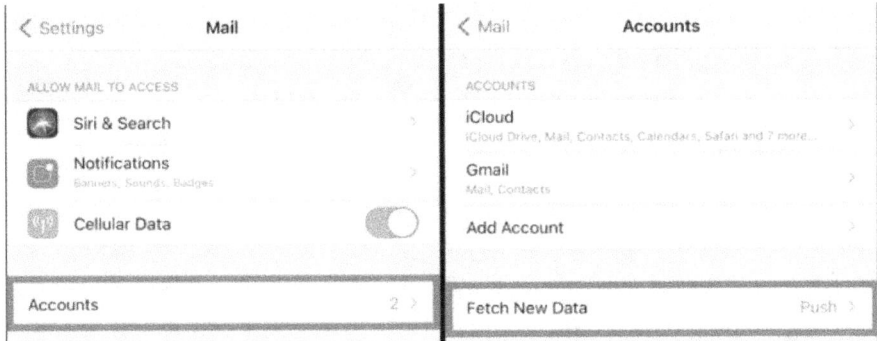

4. Managing Multiple Email Accounts

a) Switching Between Inboxes:

- Open the Mail app to view and switch between individual inboxes or see all emails aggregated in the "All Inboxes" view.

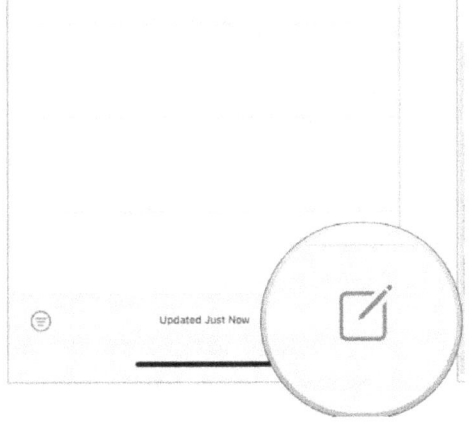

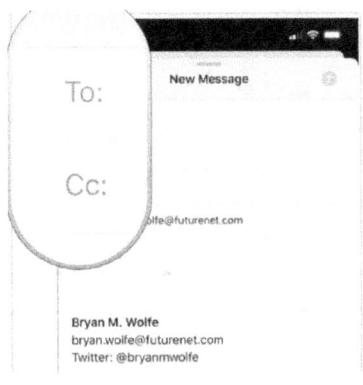

5. Sending and Receiving Emails

a) Composing Emails:

- Tap the compose button in the Mail app to write and send emails.

- Select the from address, add recipients, subject, and attach files as needed.

Chapter 4: Exploring the Web

1. Safari: Your Web Browser

a) Opening and Navigating Safari:

- Locate and open the Safari app on your home screen.

- Familiarize yourself with the user interface, including the address bar, bookmarks, tabs, and settings.

b) Searching the Web:

- Use the address bar to enter website URLs or search queries.

2. Managing Tabs and Windows

a) Opening and Closing Tabs:

- Learn how to open new tabs, close existing ones, and switch between multiple tabs for efficient browsing.

- Explore the Tab Overview screen to manage, organize, and close all open tabs at once.

b) Private Browsing:

- Understand the use of Private Browsing mode for enhanced privacy and how it differs from regular browsing.

3. Bookmarks and Reading List

a) Adding and Organizing Bookmarks:

- Bookmark your favorite websites for quick access.

- Organize bookmarks into folders and manage them through the bookmarks editor.

b) Using the Reading List:

- Add articles and web pages to your Reading List for offline reading.

- Explore automatic offline saving and organize your Reading List for convenience.

4. Navigating Web Pages

a) Zooming and Scrolling:

- Master the art of pinch-to-zoom and double-tap zooming on web pages.

- Scroll smoothly and discover the tap-to-top feature for fast navigation.

b) Reader View and Accessibility:

- Enable Reader View for a clutter-free reading experience.

- Adjust font size, style, and background color for optimal readability.

5. Autofill and Passwords

a) Setting Up Autofill:

- Configure Autofill for contact information, credit cards, and passwords under Settings > Safari > Autofill.

- Learn about the security and convenience of using Autofill.

b) Managing Saved Passwords:

- Access and manage your saved passwords using Face ID under Settings > Passwords.

6. Downloads and File Management

a) Downloading Files:

- Download files directly through Safari and access them through the Files app.

- Manage download locations and view download progress.

b) File Formats and Compatibility:

- Understand supported file formats and how to open and manage different file types on your iPhone.

7. Privacy and Security

a) Tracking Prevention and Website Settings:

- Enable or disable cross-site tracking prevention and customize settings for individual websites.

- Learn about secure website connections (HTTPS) and how to identify secure sites.

b) Clearing History and Cookies:

- Clear your browsing history, cookies, and website data for enhanced privacy.

8. Extensions and Customization

a) Installing Safari Extensions:

- Explore and install Safari Extensions from the App Store for additional functionality.

- Manage and organize your installed extensions under Settings > Safari.

b) Customizing Safari Settings:

- Tweak Safari settings for personalized browsing, including search engine selection, page zoom, and pop-up blocking.

4.1 Safari Basics

1. Launching and Using Safari

a) Opening Safari:

- Locate the Safari icon on your home screen or App Library and tap to open.

- Understand the layout of Safari, including the address bar, toolbar, and tab bar.

b) Searching and Browsing:

- Use the address bar for entering website URLs or searching the web.

- Navigate through web pages using the forward and back arrows and the swipe gesture.

2. Tabs Management

a) Opening, Closing, and Switching Tabs:

- Tap the tabs icon to open a new tab and enter a website address or search query.

- Learn how to close tabs by swiping them off the screen or using the close icon.

- Switch between open tabs by tapping on them in the tab view or using gestures.

3. Bookmarking and Reading List

a) Creating and Managing Bookmarks:

- Save your favorite websites by bookmarking them for quick access later.

- Organize your bookmarks into folders and manage them effectively.

b) Utilizing the Reading List:

- Add web pages to your Reading List for later reading, even offline.

- Explore options for managing and accessing your Reading List.

4. Navigation and Reader View

a) Scrolling and Zooming:

- Learn the basics of scrolling through web pages and using the pinch-to-zoom feature.

- Discover the 'tap to top' feature to quickly navigate to the top of a page.

b) Activating Reader View:

- Turn on Reader View for a clean and distraction-free reading experience.

- Customize the appearance of Reader View according to your preference.

5. Handling Autofill and Passwords

a) Configuring Autofill:

- Set up Safari to automatically fill in your contact information, passwords, and credit card details.

- Learn how to manage Autofill settings and ensure your information is secure.

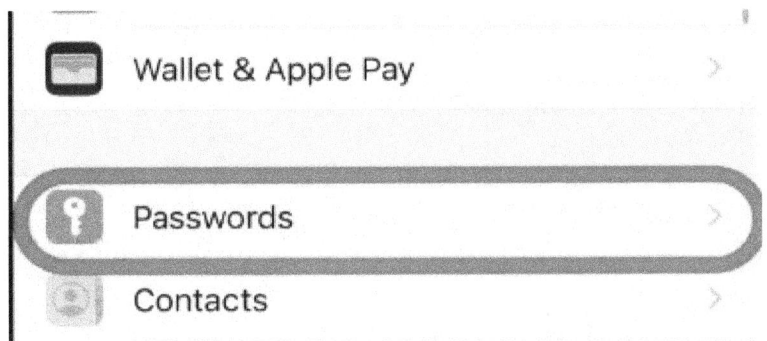

b) Managing Passwords:

- Explore how Safari can save and auto-fill passwords for websites.

- Manage your saved passwords and ensure they are secure using Face ID.

6. Downloading and Managing Files

a) Downloading Files:

- Learn how to download files directly in Safari and locate them in the Files app.

- Explore managing downloaded files and supported file formats.

b) Viewing and Sharing Downloads:

- Open and view downloaded files using appropriate apps.

7. Ensuring Privacy and Security

a) Managing Cookies and History:

- Understand the role of cookies and how to manage them for privacy.

- Learn how to clear your browsing history and website data.

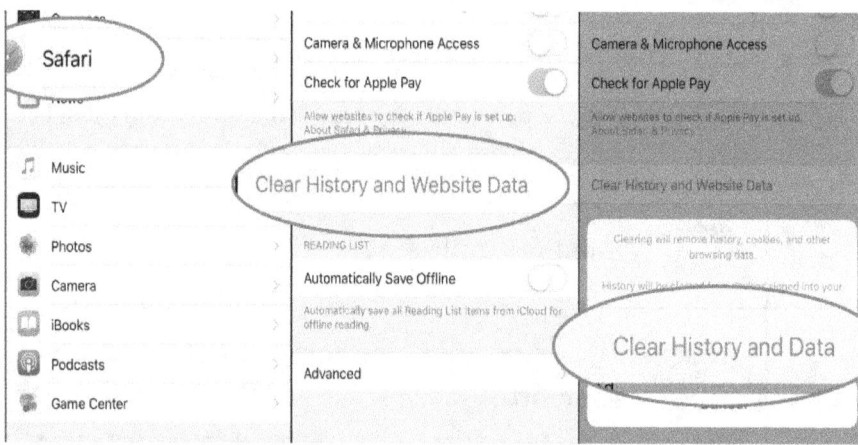

b) Browsing Securely:

- Recognize secure websites with HTTPS and understand the importance of secure browsing.

Apps

Top Categories   See All

Safari Extensions

Entertainment

Health & Fitness

Kids

Photo & Video

Productivity

Quick Links

Report a Problem

Parents' Guide to the App Store

About In-App Purchases

Apps and Games for Your Kids

About Personalization

Apps for Accessibility

Today   Games   Apps   Arcade   Search

8. Customization and Safari Extensions

a) Personalizing Safari Settings:

• Dive into Safari's settings to customize your browsing experience, including changing the default search engine, enabling pop-up blocking, and more.

b) Exploring Safari Extensions:

• Enhance Safari's functionality by exploring and installing Safari Extensions from the App Store.

• Manage your installed extensions to ensure a smooth and personalized browsing experience.

4.2 Browsing and Bookmarking Websites

1. Browsing Websites with Safari

a) Entering URLs and Searching:

• Utilize the address bar to directly input website URLs or initiate web searches.

• Explore the convenience of smart search suggestions and auto-complete features.

b) Navigating Web Pages:

- Master the navigation tools, such as the back and forward buttons, scrolling, and the swipe gesture.

- Utilize page-specific options like 'Find on Page' and 'Request Desktop Site.

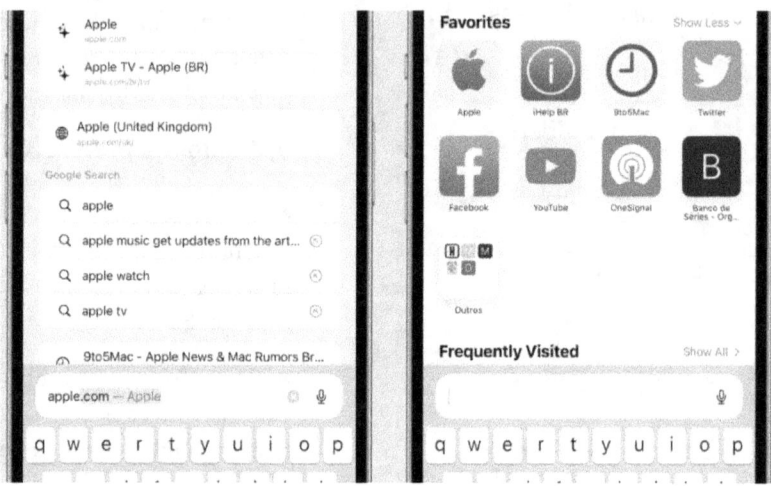

2. Opening and Managing Tabs

a) Multi-Tab Browsing:

- Learn how to open new tabs and switch between them for an organized browsing experience.

- Discover the benefits of viewing and managing tabs in landscape mode and the Tab Overview screen.

b) Closing and Reopening Tabs:

- Understand the various ways to close tabs and discover how to reopen recently closed tabs.

3. Private Browsing Mode

a) Activating and Deactivating:

- Activate Private Browsing mode for sessions where your browsing history, search history, and cookies aren't saved.

- Learn how to deactivate Private Browsing mode and understand the limitations of this feature.

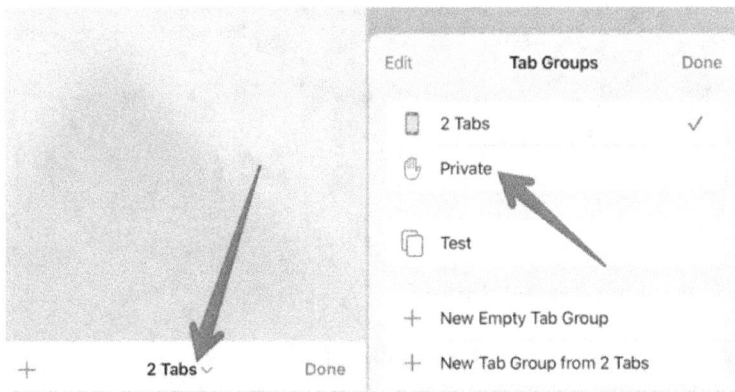

b) Privacy Considerations:

- Delve into the privacy aspects of Private Browsing and explore additional steps for enhanced digital privacy.

4. Bookmarking Your Favorite Websites

a) Creating Bookmarks:

- Bookmark your frequently visited websites for quick access.

- Customize bookmark names and choose the preferred folder for organization.

b) Managing and Editing Bookmarks:

- Explore the Bookmarks menu to manage, edit, and organize your collection.

- Learn how to create bookmark folders, rearrange bookmarks, and edit details.

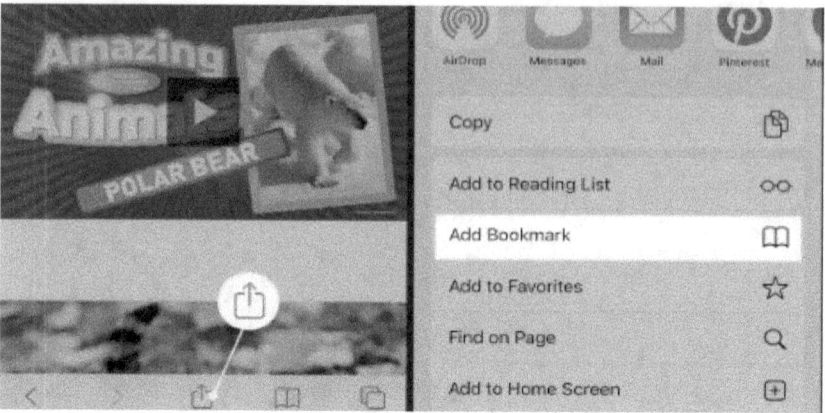

5. Curating Your Reading List

a) Adding and Accessing Reading List:

- Save articles and web pages to your Reading List for later or offline reading.

- Access and manage your Reading List with ease, and explore options for offline reading.

b) Organizing and Deleting Items:

- Learn the various ways to organize items in your Reading List.

- Discover how to delete items individually or clear your entire Reading List.

6. Sharing and Saving Web Content

a) Using the Share Sheet:

- Explore the versatility of the Share Sheet for sending web content via messages, email, or social media.

- Learn how to save images, documents, and other web content to your device.

b) Other Saving Options:

- Discover alternative ways to save web content, including PDF creation and printing options.

7. Syncing Bookmarks and Reading List Across Devices

a) Enabling iCloud Sync:

- Ensure iCloud is configured to sync your Bookmarks and Reading List across your Apple devices.

- Access and manage synchronized content on different devices seamlessly.

b) Managing Sync Settings:

- Delve into iCloud settings to manage synchronization options and ensure a consistent browsing experience across devices.

4.3 Online Safety Tips

1. Safeguarding Personal Information

a) Strong, Unique Passwords:

- Create robust and unique passwords for your online accounts.
- Use a mix of letters, numbers, and symbols to enhance security.

2. Recognizing and Avoiding Phishing Scams

a) Identifying Phishing Attempts:

- Learn to recognize suspicious emails, messages, and websites.
- Avoid clicking on unknown links and verify the authenticity of contact requests and communications.

b) Reporting Phishing:

- Report phishing attempts to your email provider or the legitimate entity being impersonated.
- Utilize built-in browser features to report suspicious websites.

3. Browsing Securely with Safari

a) HTTPS and SSL Certificates:

- Prioritize websites using HTTPS for secure, encrypted connections.
- Learn how to identify websites with valid SSL certificates and the signs of a secure connection.

b) Privacy and Tracking Protection:

- Enable Safari's privacy features, including cross-site tracking prevention and intelligent tracking protection.
- Manage cookies and website data to safeguard your online privacy.

4. Using Public Wi-Fi Wisely

a) Risks of Public Wi-Fi:

- Avoid accessing sensitive information or conducting financial transactions on public networks.

b) VPN for Enhanced Security:

- Explore Virtual Private Network (VPN) options for secure browsing on public networks.

- Learn how to set up and use a VPN on your iPhone 15.

5. Regularly Updating Software

a) Importance of Updates:

- Understand the significance of keeping your iPhone 15 and apps up to date.

- Regularly check for and install software updates to patch vulnerabilities and enhance security.

b) Managing Update Settings:

- Customize your update settings and enable automatic updates for convenience and security.

6. Backing Up Important Data

a) Utilizing iCloud Backup:

- Set up and use iCloud Backup to regularly back up your important data.

- Manage your iCloud storage and backup settings for optimal use.

b) Alternative Backup Options:

- Explore alternative options for backing up your iPhone, including iTunes and third-party solutions.

Chapter 5: Apps for Everyday

1. Productivity Powerhouses

a) Calendar and Reminders:

- Learn to organize your schedule, set appointments, and manage tasks using the Calendar and Reminders apps.

- Explore syncing options and notification settings for staying on top of your commitments.

b) Notes and Documents:

- Dive into the Notes app for jotting down ideas, creating checklists, and sketching.

- Explore document scanning, organizing notes, and using third-party document apps for added functionality.

2. Staying Connected and Informed

a) Messages and FaceTime:

- Master the art of communication using Messages for texting and FaceTime for video calls.

- Explore features like group chats, Memoji, effects, and end-to-end encryption for secure conversations.

b) Mail and Safari:

- Manage your email efficiently using the Mail app and explore customization options.

- Navigate the web seamlessly with Safari, understanding bookmarks, reading lists, and privacy settings.

3. Health and Wellness Companions

a) Health and Fitness Apps:

- Discover the Health app's capabilities in tracking and managing your health data and fitness activities.

- Explore a range of fitness apps for workouts, meditation, nutrition, and sleep tracking.

b) Mindfulness and Meditation Apps:

- Delve into apps that promote mindfulness, relaxation, and mental well-being.

- Learn about different meditation techniques, guided sessions, and personalized mindfulness programs.

4. Entertainment and Leisure

a) Music and Podcasts:

- Navigate the Music app, exploring libraries, playlists, and discovering new tunes.

- Delve into the world of podcasts, finding your favorites, subscribing, and managing episodes.

b) Games and Streaming Services:

- Explore the vast array of games available on the App Store, from casual to hardcore gaming experiences.

- Discover popular streaming services for movies, TV shows, and live events, comparing features and content libraries.

5. Learning and Development

a) Educational Apps and eBooks:

- Explore educational apps for learning new skills, languages, and subjects.

- Dive into the world of eBooks, exploring reading apps, and discovering a vast library of digital books.

b) Creativity and Design Apps:

- Unleash your creativity with apps for drawing, designing, photo editing, and video creation.

- Discover tutorials and resources for honing your creative skills and sharing your work.

6. Lifestyle and Utility Apps

a) Shopping and Finance Apps:

- Navigate shopping apps for best deals, secure payments, and efficient order tracking.

- Manage your finances using budgeting, investing, and banking apps with security features.

b) Travel and Navigation Apps:

- Explore travel apps for booking flights, accommodations, and planning itineraries.

- Master navigation apps for maps, traffic updates, public transit information, and location sharing.

7. Customizing Your App Experience

a) Organizing and Managing Apps:

- Learn the best practices for organizing apps, creating folders, and managing app pages.

- Explore settings for app updates, notifications, and background app refresh for optimal performance.

b) Discovering New Apps:

- Navigate the App Store efficiently to discover new apps, read reviews, and compare similar apps.

- Understand app permissions, subscriptions, and in-app purchases for a secure and informed app experience.

5.1 Health and Accessibility

Health App

1. All-in-One Health Data Management

- Complete Health Monitoring: A versatile platform that logs and examines various health-related data such as step count and sleep quality.

- Integration with Fitness Devices: Seamlessly connects with a range of fitness devices and applications, centralizing all health-related metrics.

- Emergency Medical ID: Stores vital health information for quick access from the lock screen during emergencies.

2. Comprehensive Activity and Fitness Tracking

- Advanced Motion Sensing: Utilizes the iPhone's built-in sensors to accurately track activities like walking, running, and stair climbing.

3. Digital Usage and Wellness Supervision

- Screen Time Analysis: Tracks and analyzes device usage, enabling users to set limits on app usage for a balanced digital life.

- Downtime Scheduling: Facilitates scheduled breaks from technology, promoting mental health and digital detox.

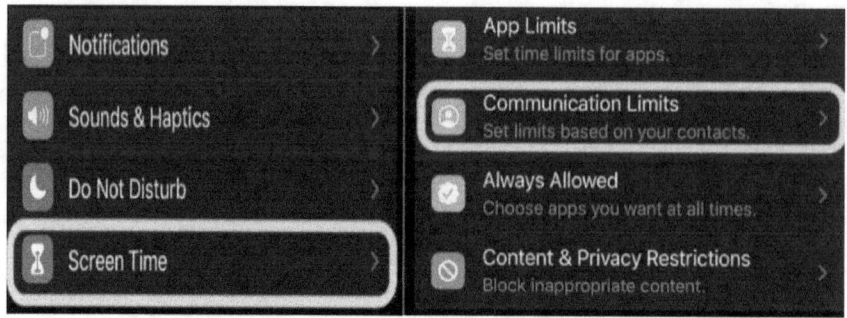

4. Sleep Tracking and Wind Down

- Analyze sleep patterns and set bedtime schedules for a consistent sleep routine.

- Wind Down mode prepares you for bedtime, reducing screen brightness and limiting notifications.

5. Accessibility for the Visually Impaired

- VoiceOver: A gesture-based screen reader that offers spoken feedback.

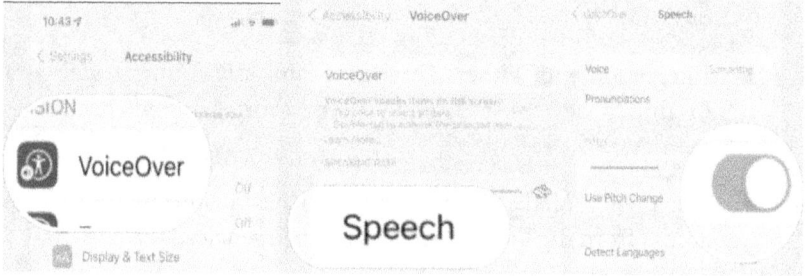

- Magnifier: Use the iPhone's camera to magnify text or objects.

- Display Accommodations: Adjust screen settings like color inversions or contrasts to enhance readability.

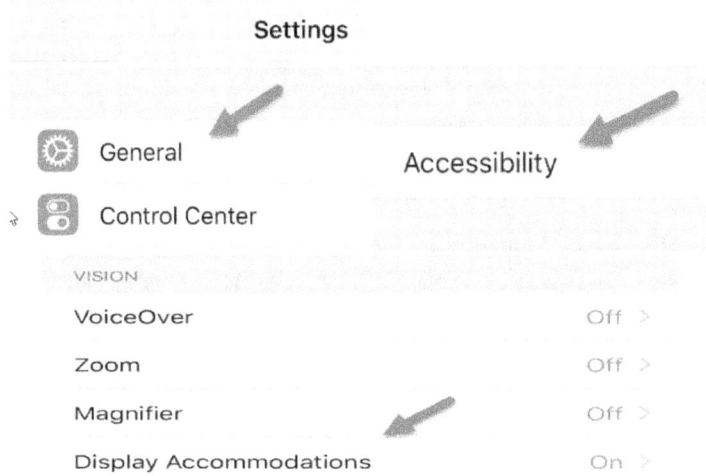

6. Enhanced Accessibility Features for Hearing Impairment

- Live Listen: This feature enhances real-world sounds when using AirPods or compatible hearing devices, making it easier for users with hearing impairments.

- Visual Alerts: Transforms sound notifications into LED flash or on-screen visual signals, aiding those who are hard of hearing.

- Mono Audio and Balance Adjustment: Tailors audio output for users with unilateral hearing loss, ensuring a balanced and clear audio experience.

7. Emergency SOS Functionality

- Quick Activation: A simple gesture quickly contacts emergency services and alerts pre-selected emergency contacts.

- Auto-call Option: This can be activated for situations where speaking is not feasible, ensuring timely assistance.

8. Privacy in Health Data Management

- Secure Data Handling: Apple prioritizes user privacy by encrypting all health data and requiring user permission for data sharing.

- App Access Control: Users can manage which apps can access their health metrics, enhancing privacy and security.

9. Participation in Health Research

- Research Contribution: Users can voluntarily participate in medical research studies through their iPhone, ensuring anonymity and contributing to healthcare advancements.

10. Diverse Health and Accessibility Apps

- Extensive App Selection: The App Store offers a wide range of apps focused on specific health and accessibility needs.

- Variety of Apps: Includes meditation apps like Headspace and specialized communication tools such as Proloquo2Go, catering to diverse user requirements.

5.2 Health App Overview

1. Dashboard

- The "Summary" tab provides an overview of your health metrics, spotlighting data like steps, heart rate, sleep, and more.

- Customize what you see for a tailored view of your most pertinent information.

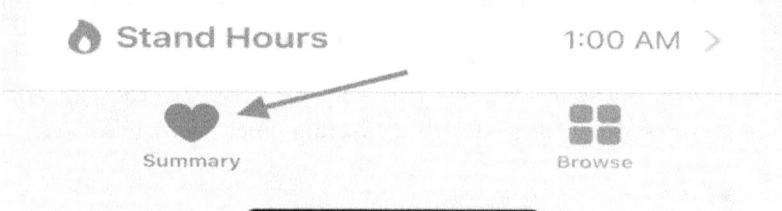

2. Health Categories

- Dive deeper into a wide array of health metrics, from activity and mindfulness to nutrition and reproductive health.

- Track specific details, whether it's dietary intake, menstrual cycles, or meditation minutes.

3. Data Sources and Access

- View and manage the apps and devices contributing data to the Health app.

- Prioritize sources and decide which apps can access specific health information.

4. Medical ID: A Lifesaver

- Store critical medical information like allergies, medications, blood type, and emergency contacts.

- Accessible from the lock screen, it can be invaluable to first responders in emergencies.

5. Health Records: Integration with Medical Institutions

- For participating medical institutions, integrate your official medical records directly into the Health app.

- View lab results, immunizations, diagnoses, and more, all in one organized space.

6. Trends and Highlights

- Based on your health data, the app provides insights and trends over time.

- Monitor changes, track progress, or identify areas requiring attention.

7. Sharing Health Data

- Opt to share specific health metrics with family, caregivers, or medical professionals.

- Provides a way for loved ones or healthcare providers to stay informed, especially valuable for those in eldercare or with specific medical conditions.

8. Health Checklist

- A guide to set up and optimize various health and safety features, from Medical ID to Emergency SOS.

9. Research and Participation

- Contribute to health studies directly via the app, aiding medical research.

- Participation is voluntary, with data privacy and anonymity maintained.

5.3 Fitness Tracking

As we age, staying active and monitoring our fitness becomes increasingly important. The Health App on the iPhone 15 offers seniors a personalized and accessible way to track their fitness activities, encouraging a healthy and active lifestyle. This chapter will guide seniors through utilizing the Health App for keeping tabs on their fitness journey.

1. Embracing Activity with the Health App

- **Getting Started**

The Health App simplifies the process of monitoring various types of physical activities, from walking to swimming. To start, seniors can input basic health information such as age, weight, and height to tailor the activity tracking to their specific needs.

- **Understanding the Activity Rings**

The iPhone 15 displays activity data in three rings: Move, Exercise, and Stand. These rings provide a visual and straightforward way for seniors to track their daily activity levels.

Move Ring: Tracks the active calories burned throughout the day.
Exercise Ring: Monitors the amount of brisk activity undertaken.
Stand Ring: Reminds users to stand and move around regularly to avoid long periods of inactivity.

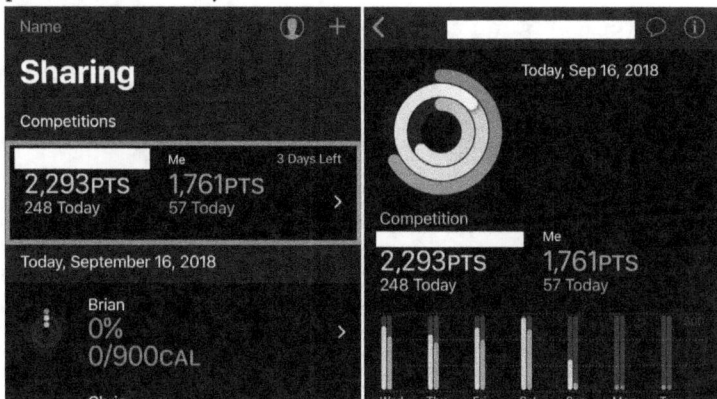

- **Customizing Goals**

Seniors can personalize their Move goals based on their ability and comfort levels. The app allows for weekly goal adjustments, ensuring that the targets are flexible and adaptable to the senior's changing fitness levels.

2. Monitoring Workouts

- **Recording Exercises**

The Health App provides options to log a variety of workouts, catering to different interests and capabilities, whether it's a leisurely walk in the park or a yoga session.

- **Visualizing Progress**

Through the app, seniors can see detailed summaries of their workouts, including duration, heart rate, and distance. This feedback is crucial for understanding their progress and motivating them to continue.

3. Strength Training and Indoor Workouts

- Explore apps and tools designed for gym-goers, including weight tracking, repetition counting, and rest timers.

- The role of third-party wearables in tracking heart rate, calories burned, and workout intensity.

4. Encouraging Regular

- **Movement Stand and Move Alerts**

The iPhone 15 can be set to send reminders to stand up or move if the user has been sedentary for too long. These nudges are helpful for maintaining consistent activity throughout the day.

- **Mobility Tracking**

The Health App also tracks mobility data such as walking speed, step length, and walking asymmetry, which are important indicators of a senior's overall physical condition and balance.

5. Celebrating

- **Achievements Sharing Success**

Seniors can share their activity accomplishments with friends and family through the app, fostering a sense of community and shared progress.

- **Awards and Milestones**

The Health App encourages continued activity by offering rewards for reaching milestones, turning fitness into a rewarding experience.

6. Safety and Privacy

- **Emergency SOS**

The iPhone 15 includes an Emergency SOS feature that seniors can use if they need immediate help during their fitness activities.

- **Privacy Assurance**

All health data tracked by the app is encrypted and stored securely, with the senior maintaining full control over their information.

Fitness tracking for seniors on the iPhone 15 is more than just counting steps—it's about encouraging a healthier, more active lifestyle. The Health App serves as a companion in this journey, offering tailored tracking, motivational incentives, and the assurance of safety and privacy. With these tools, seniors are empowered to take charge of their fitness and enjoy the benefits of an active life.

5.4 Control of Taking Pills in Health app

The Health App on the iPhone 15 is not just a tool for tracking physical activity and fitness; it also serves as a vigilant assistant for medication management. This chapter will focus exclusively on how to use the Health App to control and track your pill intake, ensuring you stay on top of your medication regimen.

1. Setting Up Your Medication List

- **Adding Medications**

Begin by launching the Health App and navigate to the 'Health Records' section. Here, you can add each medication you take, along with details such as strength and dosage form.

- **Customizing Dosage and Schedule**

For each medication, you can input the specific dosage and the frequency at which it needs to be taken. Whether it's a one-time dose or a complex schedule, the Health App can accommodate various regimens.

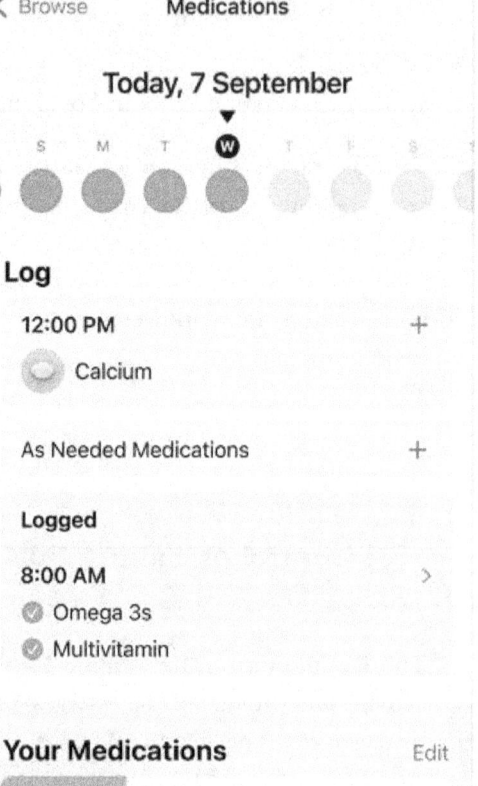

2. Managing Your Intake

- **Reminders and Alerts**

Once your medications are logged, you can set up reminders. These notifications will alert you when it's time to take your next dose, ensuring you never miss a pill.

- **Intake Logging**

After taking your medication, you can log this in the app, which helps maintain an accurate record of your intake. This log can be invaluable during doctor visits or in emergency situations.

3. Sharing with Healthcare Providers

- **Exporting Data**

The Health App allows you to export your medication logs, which can be shared with your healthcare provider for review during appointments, aiding in discussions about your treatment plan.

- · **Privacy and Security**

With the sensitive nature of health data, the iPhone 15 ensures that your medication information is securely stored and encrypted. You have control over who this information is shared with.

4. Advanced Features

- **Drug Interaction Warnings**

The Health App can alert you to potential drug interactions based on the medication list you've entered, helping you avoid adverse effects.

- **Refill Reminders**

For medications you take regularly, the app can also remind you when it's time to refill your prescription, so you're never without your necessary medication.

- **Visual Aids**

For those who take multiple medications, the app can use images of the pills, which can be a helpful visual aid to ensure you're taking the right medication at the right time.

5.5 Entertainment Apps

1. Music and Audio

a) Apple Music:

- Dive into the rich music library, explore playlists, discover new artists, and curate your musical universe.

- Understand subscription plans, offline listening, and how to create and share your playlists.

b) Podcasts and Audiobooks:

- Explore the wide range of podcasts across genres and audiobooks from various platforms.

- Learn about subscribing, downloading for offline access, and customizing your listening experience.

2. Movies, TV Shows, and Streaming

a) Apple TV and Streaming Services:

- Navigate through Apple TV and an array of streaming services like

Netflix　　　　　Hulu　　　　and Disney+　　　.

- Compare subscriptions, explore content libraries, and understand viewing preferences and recommendations.

b) Video Platforms:

- Dive into popular video platforms like YouTube 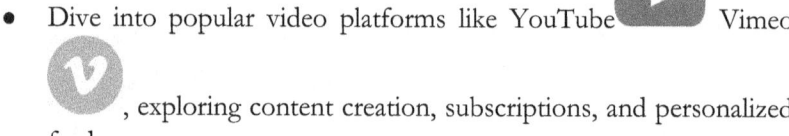 Vimeo , exploring content creation, subscriptions, and personalized feeds.
- Understand video uploading, commenting, liking, and sharing functionalities.

3. Gaming Universe

a) App Store Games:

- Discover the gaming paradise of Apple Arcade, exploring a variety of games across genres.

b) Top 10 Games for seniors:

- **Words With Friends 2:** A word puzzle game that is great for keeping the mind sharp. It also offers a social aspect, as players can connect and play with friends and family.

- **Sudoku:** This classic number puzzle game is excellent for stimulating the brain and improving problem-solving skills.

- **Solitaire:** A timeless card game that is perfect for relaxation and can be played at a comfortable pace.

- **Candy Crush Saga:** A fun and colorful match-three puzzle game that's easy to learn but challenging to master.

- **Crossword Puzzles:** Ideal for word enthusiasts, these puzzles come in varying difficulties and are great for vocabulary and memory.

- **Mahjong Solitaire:** A tile-matching game that requires strategic thinking and concentration, good for keeping the mind active.

- **Jigsaw Puzzle:** This app offers a digital jigsaw puzzle experience, which is great for cognitive health and can be adjusted in terms of difficulty.

- **Brain Training Games:** Apps like Lumosity or Peak offer a variety of brain training games designed to enhance cognitive functions like memory, attention, and problem-solving.

- **2048:** A simple yet addictive puzzle game that challenges players to slide numbered tiles and combine them to reach the number 2048.

- **Bejeweled Classic:** Another match-three puzzle game, known for its relaxing effects and visually appealing graphics.

4. Social Media and Communication

a) Social Media Platforms:

- Navigate through popular social media apps like Instagram, Facebook, Twitter, and Snapchat.

- Explore posting, commenting, direct messaging, and understanding privacy settings and notifications.

b) Messaging and Video Call Apps:

- Stay connected through messaging apps like WhatsApp and Messenger, exploring texting, voice messages, and group chats.

- Dive into video calling with apps like Zoom and FaceTime, understanding features and settings.

5. Books and Comics

a) E-Books and Reading Apps:

- Discover the joy of reading with apps like Apple Books and Kindle, exploring vast libraries and reading options.

- Learn about purchasing, downloading, and customizing your reading experience.

6. Creative Outlets

a) Photography and Video Editing:

- Unleash your creativity with photo and video editing apps like Adobe Lightroom and iMovie.

- Explore editing tools, filters, and sharing your creations on social media.

b) Art and Design Apps:

- Dive into digital art with apps like Procreate and Adobe Sketch, exploring tools and techniques.

- Learn about digital drawing, design principles, and sharing your artwork online.

7. News and Magazines

a) News Apps and Aggregators:

- Stay informed with news apps like Apple News and aggregators like Flipboard.

- Customize your news feed, explore categories, and understand subscription options.

b) Magazines and Specialized Publications:

- Explore digital magazines and specialized publications across genres and interests.

5.6 Utility Apps

1. Organization and Task Management

a) Notes and Reminders:

- Discover the functionalities of Apple Notes and Reminders for jotting down thoughts and setting up to-do lists.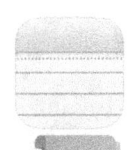

- Learn about organizing notes, setting reminders, and syncing across devices.

b) Third-Party Task Managers:

- Explore popular task management apps like Todoist and Microsoft To-Do for advanced organization.

- Understand features like project organization, collaboration, and priority setting.

2. File Management and Storage

a) Files App and iCloud Drive :

- Navigate the Files app and iCloud for storing, organizing, and accessing documents.

- Learn about file sharing, folder organization, and managing iCloud storage.

b) Third-Party Cloud Storage:

- Explore other cloud storage options like Google Drive and Dropbox.

- Understand storage plans, file sharing, and collaboration features.

3. Calculators and Converters

a) Calculator App:

- Familiarize yourself with the built-in Calculator app and its functionalities.

- Learn tips and tricks for scientific calculations and unit conversions.

b) Currency and Unit Converters:

- Explore apps for converting currencies and units, such as XE Currency and Unit Converter.

- Understand real-time exchange rates, offline mode, and customization.

4. Scanning and Printing

a) Document Scanners:

- Discover the scanning functionalities within the Notes app and third-party apps like CamScanner.

- Learn about scanning quality, editing scans, and sharing scanned documents.

b) Printing Apps:

- Explore options for wireless printing through apps like Printer Pro.

- Understand printer compatibility, print settings, and troubleshooting.

5. Navigation and Weather

a) Maps and GPS Apps:

- Navigate the features of Apple Maps and explore alternatives like Google Maps and Waze.

- Learn about real-time navigation, traffic updates, and location sharing.

b) Weather Apps:

- Familiarize yourself with the Apple Weather app and explore alternatives like Dark Sky.

- Understand weather forecasts, alerts, and customization features.

6. Productivity Tools

a) Office Suites and PDF Editors:

- Explore office suite apps like Microsoft Office and Google Workspace for document creation and editing.

- Learn about PDF editors like Adobe Acrobat for annotating and signing documents.

b) Email and Calendar Apps:

- Navigate through email apps like Apple Mail and alternatives like Gmail.

Chapter 6: Camera and Photo

1. Exploring the Camera App

a) Navigating the Interface:

- Familiarize yourself with the Camera app's interface, including shutter button, mode selector, and settings.

- Discover the various shooting modes, such as Photo, Video, Portrait, Pano, and more.

b) Understanding Camera Settings:

- Delve into camera settings to adjust resolution, frame rate, and formats.

- Explore features like Live Photo, HDR, Night mode, and Deep Fusion for enhanced photography.

2. Advanced Shooting Techniques

a) Utilizing Optical and Digital Zoom:

- Understand the differences between optical and digital zoom and how to use them effectively.

- Learn how to achieve the best quality when zooming in on subjects.

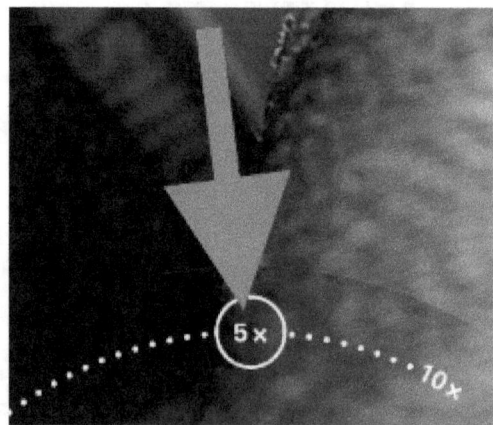

b) Mastering Portrait Mode:

- Discover the art of taking stunning portraits with background blur (bokeh).

- Explore different lighting effects and depth control for professional-looking portraits.

3. Editing and Enhancing Photos

a) Using the Photos App for Editing:

- Navigate the editing tools in the Photos app to enhance your images.

- Adjust light, color, crop, filter, and more to perfect your shots.

b) Exploring Advanced Editing Options:

- Dive into advanced editing features, such as retouching, selective adjustments, and markup.

- Discover third-party photo editing apps for additional creative possibilities.

4. Organizing and Managing Your Photos

a) Creating Albums and Folders:

- Learn how to organize your photos into albums and folders for easy access.

- Explore smart albums and how to customize your album structure.

b) Utilizing Search and Memories:

- Use the powerful search feature to find photos by people, places, objects, and more.

- Discover the Memories feature for reliving and sharing your favorite moments.

5. Sharing and Backing Up Your Memories

a) Sharing Photos and Albums:

- Explore the various ways to share photos and albums, including AirDrop, Messages, Mail, and social media.

- Learn how to create shared albums for collaborative photo collections.

b) Backing Up to iCloud Photos:

- Set up iCloud Photos for syncing and backing up your entire photo library across devices.

- Understand iCloud storage plans and how to manage your storage efficiently.

6. Exploring Additional Photography Apps

a) Third-Party Camera Apps:

- Discover popular third-party camera apps for additional shooting modes and controls.

- Learn how to use manual controls for exposure, focus, white balance, and more.

b) Creative Photo Editing Apps:

- Explore a range of photo editing apps for creative effects, advanced retouching, and artistic expression.

- Find the right apps to complement your photography style and needs.

7. Printing and Creating Photo Products

a) Printing Photos:

- Discover options for printing photos directly from your iPhone.

- Explore online printing services and local printing solutions.

b) Creating Custom Photo Products:

- Learn how to create custom photo products, such as photo books, calendars, and wall art.

- Explore various platforms and services for designing and ordering personalized photo gifts.

6.1 Taking Pictures and Videos

1. Mastering the Art of Composition

a) Rule of Thirds:

- **Understand the basics of the Rule of Thirds and how it can enhance your compositions.**

Is a photography technique that helps you create balanced and interesting compositions by dividing your image into nine equal parts with two horizontal and two vertical lines. The idea is to place the main subject or elements of your photo along these lines or at their intersections, rather than in the center of the frame. This way, you can create more dynamic and visually appealing images that draw the viewer's attention.

If you want to use the rule of thirds on your iPhone 15, you can enable the camera grid in your Settings app. The grid will overlay on your camera screen and help you align your shots with the rule of thirds. Here are the steps to turn on the grid on your iPhone 15:

- **Open the Settings app.**

- **Tap Camera.**

- **Find Grid and toggle it on.**

- **Return to the Camera app; you'll see a faint grid over the capture frame.**

- **Learn to use the grid feature on your iPhone to frame your shots effectively.**

b) Finding the Right Angle and Perspective:

- Experiment with different angles and perspectives to bring uniqueness to your shots.

2. Harnessing Natural Light

a) Understanding Lighting:

- Learn the impact of different lighting conditions on your photos and videos.

- Discover tips for shooting in low light, backlit scenarios, and harsh sunlight.

b) Using Flash Wisely:

- Understand when to use the flash and how it affects your photos.

- Explore the slow sync flash feature for better results in low light.

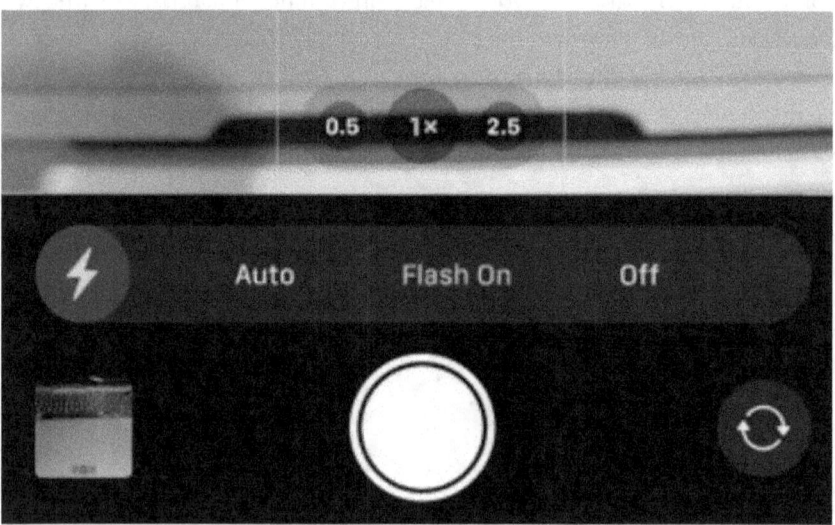

3. Capturing Photos in Various Modes

a) Utilizing Photo Mode:

- Explore the standard Photo mode and learn tips for taking sharp, well-balanced pictures.

- Understand the impact of HDR and how to use it effectively.

b) Experimenting with Portrait and Pano Modes:

- Dive into the Portrait mode to create professional-looking portraits with depth effects.

- Learn how to capture stunning panoramic shots using the Pano mode.

4. Shooting Videos Like a Pro

a) Exploring Slo-mo and Time-lapse:

- Discover the creative possibilities of shooting in Slo-mo and Time-lapse modes.

- Learn tips and techniques for achieving the best results in these modes.

5. Using Live Photos and QuickTake

a) Capturing Live Photos:

- Learn how to capture moments with sound and motion using Live Photos.

- Discover creative ways to use and edit Live Photos.

b) QuickTake for Instant Video Recording:

- Understand how to use QuickTake for capturing videos without switching out of Photo mode.

- Learn scenarios where QuickTake can be especially handy.

6. Focusing and Exposure Adjustment

a) Manual Focus and Exposure Control:

- Explore how to manually adjust focus and exposure for the perfect shot.

- Learn to use AE/AF Lock for maintaining consistent settings across shots.

b) Using Exposure Compensation Control:

- Understand how to use the exposure compensation control for adjusting brightness.

- Learn scenarios where adjusting exposure can enhance your shots.

7. Exploring Filters and Effects

a) Applying Filters:

- Discover the variety of built-in filters and how they can transform your photos and videos.

- Learn to apply filters both before and after capturing.

b) Creative Effects:

- Explore additional creative effects, such as lens flare, vignette, and slow shutter.

- Learn how to use these effects to add a touch of creativity to your visuals.

6.2 Editing and Organizing Your Memories

1. Unleashing the Power of Photo Editing

a) Basic Adjustments:

- Explore the foundational editing tools: cropping, rotating, and straightening.

- Dive into adjustments for light and color, including exposure, brightness, contrast, and saturation.

b) Advanced Editing Techniques:

- Uncover the advanced capabilities: selective adjustments, retouching, and gradient filters.

- Experiment with creative edits using features like vignette, grain, and fade.

2. Enhancing Videos with Precision

a) Trimming and Adjusting Videos:

- Learn the essentials of video editing: trimming, splitting, and adjusting the frame.

- Explore adjustments for color balance, exposure, and highlights/shadows.

b) Adding Effects and Transitions:

- Discover how to incorporate effects, filters, and transitions for dynamic video storytelling.

- Experiment with slow motion, reverse, and time-lapse for creative video sequences.

3. Mastering the Art of Organization

a) Creating Albums and Folders:

- Establish a systematic approach to organizing your photos and videos into albums and folders.

- Learn the benefits of creating Smart Albums and utilizing the Favorites album.

b) Utilizing Search and Sorting:

- Harness the power of intelligent search features to locate memories based on people, places, and objects.

- Understand various sorting options for viewing your collection in a way that suits you.

4. Harnessing the Capabilities of Memories

a) Exploring the Memories Feature:

- Dive into the Memories feature to relive and rediscover moments in a cinematic presentation.

- Learn how to customize Memories with different moods, music, and durations.

b) Sharing and Saving Memories:

- Discover the various sharing options for your curated Memories.

- Learn how to save and export Memories for preservation and external sharing.

5. Managing Storage and Backup Solutions

a) Optimizing iPhone Storage:

- Understand how to manage and optimize your iPhone storage for photos and videos.

- Explore options for offloading unused apps and clearing temporary files.

b) iCloud and Alternative Backup Solutions:

- Set up and manage iCloud for seamless photo and video backup across devices.

- Explore alternative backup solutions, including physical storage and third-party cloud services.

6. Curating and Sharing Your Visual Stories

a) Creating Shared Albums:

- Learn how to create and manage Shared Albums for collaborative photo and video collections.

- Discover ways to invite contributors, manage permissions, and interact with shared content.

b) Exporting and Sharing Creatives:

- Explore various exporting options and file formats for sharing your edited creatives.

- Learn the best practices for sharing high-quality visuals through different platforms.

7. Third-Party Editing Apps and Tools

a) Exploring App Store Gems:

- Discover popular third-party photo and video editing apps available on the App Store.

- Experiment with different apps to find the ones that align with your creative vision and editing needs.

b) Integrating External Editing Solutions:

- Learn how to integrate external editing solutions and plugins for a diversified editing experience.

- Explore workflow optimizations by incorporating third-party tools into your editing process.

Chapter 7: Personalizing Your iPhone

1. Changing Wallpaper and Display Settings

a) Wallpaper:

- Navigate to Settings > Wallpaper to select from dynamic, still, or live wallpapers, or choose an image from your Photos.

- Customize your Lock Screen and Home Screen with different images for a diversified look.

b) Display Settings:

- Adjust the brightness, text size, and view (Standard or Zoomed) under Settings > Display & Brightness.

- Activate Dark Mode or set it to turn on automatically based on time or ambient light conditions.

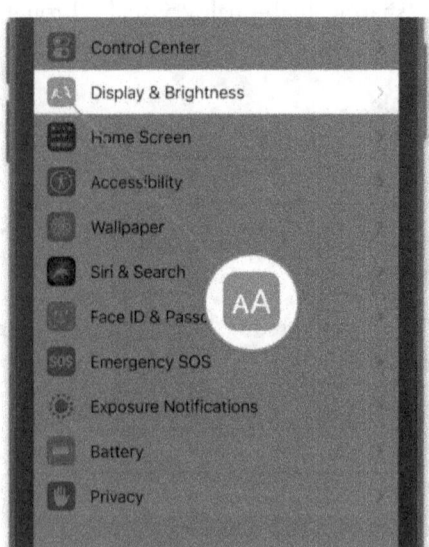 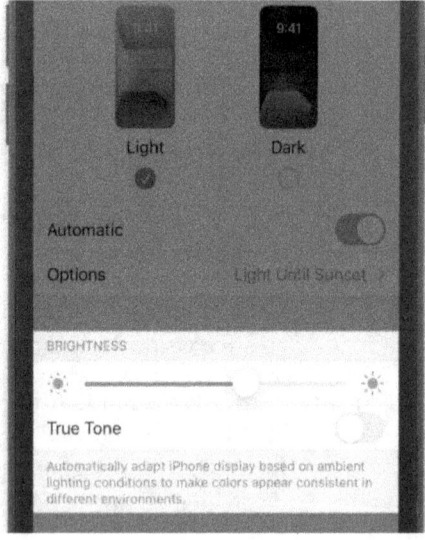

2. Organizing Apps and Home Screen

a) App Arrangement:

- Touch and hold any app icon until it jiggles, then drag it to a new location or a different Home Screen page.

- Drag an app onto another app to create a folder. Name the folder or use the suggested name based on the apps' category.

b) App Library:

- Utilize the App Library to categorize your apps automatically.

- Choose which Home Screen pages to display by tapping on the page dots at the bottom and selecting Edit Pages.

3. Customizing Control Center

- Go to Settings > Control Center to add, remove, or rearrange controls.

- Customize the included controls like Flashlight, Timer, Calculator, and Camera for quick access to functionalities.

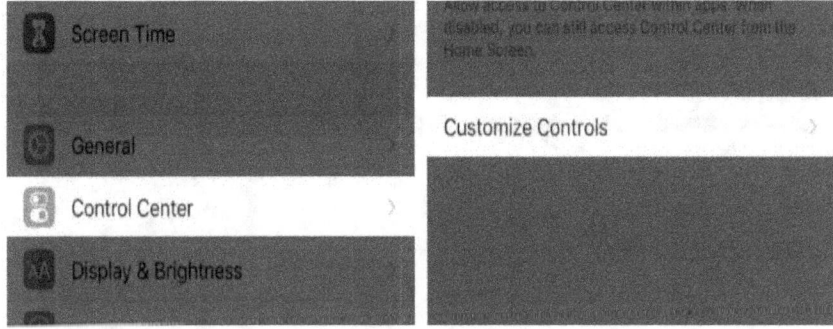

4. Personalizing Sounds and Haptics

a) Ringtones and Alert Tones:

- Set a unique ringtone, text tone, and other alert tones under Settings > Sounds & Haptics.

b) Haptic Feedback:

- Customize the haptic feedback for system controls and interactions under Settings > Sounds & Haptics > System Haptics.

5. Setting Up Accessibility Features

- Explore and enable features under Settings > Accessibility to personalize your iPhone based on your needs and preferences.

- Customize VoiceOver, Zoom, Magnifier, and other accessibility features for enhanced usability.

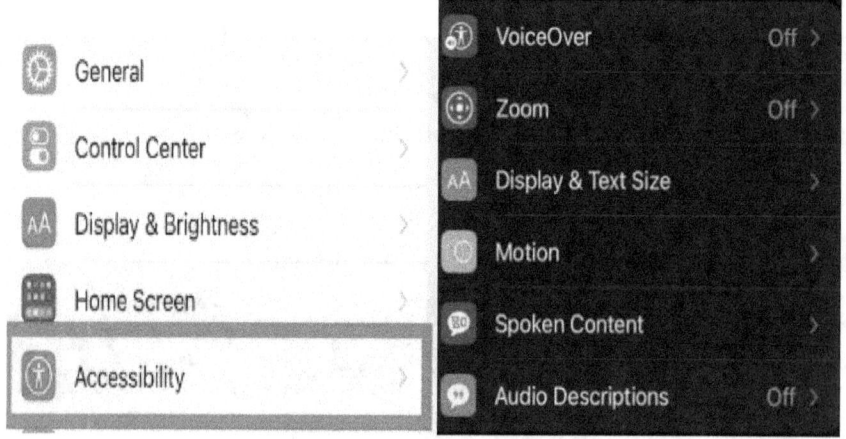

6. Siri and Shortcuts

a) Siri:

- Personalize Siri's voice, language, and responses under Settings > Siri & Search.

- Enable or disable "Hey Siri" and customize your Siri Suggestions.

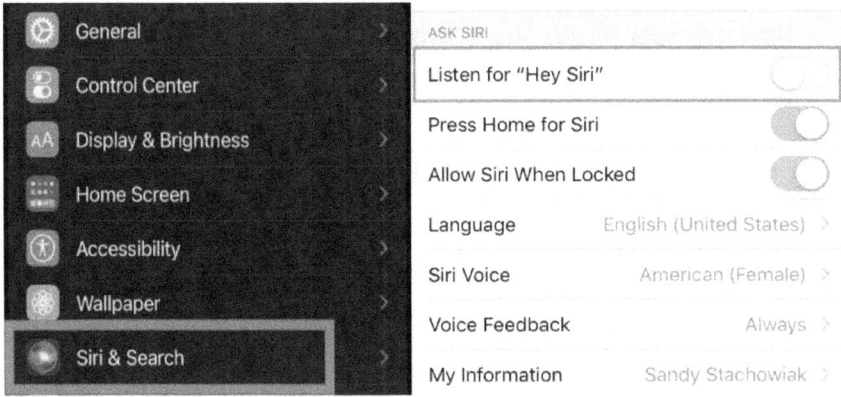

b) Shortcuts:

- Create personalized shortcuts for automating tasks under the Shortcuts app.

- Customize your shortcuts based on your daily routines and frequently used apps.

7. Privacy Settings

- Customize your privacy settings under Settings > Privacy to manage location services, tracking, app permissions, and more.

8. Widget Customization

- Press and hold an empty space on the Home Screen to add or customize widgets.

- Choose from different widget sizes and arrange them based on your preferences for at-a-glance information.

7.1 Setting Up Your Wallpaper

1. Choosing Your Wallpaper

a) Pre-Installed Options:

- Navigate to Settings > Wallpaper > Choose a New Wallpaper.

- Explore Dynamic, Stills, and Live categories, each offering a unique visual experience.

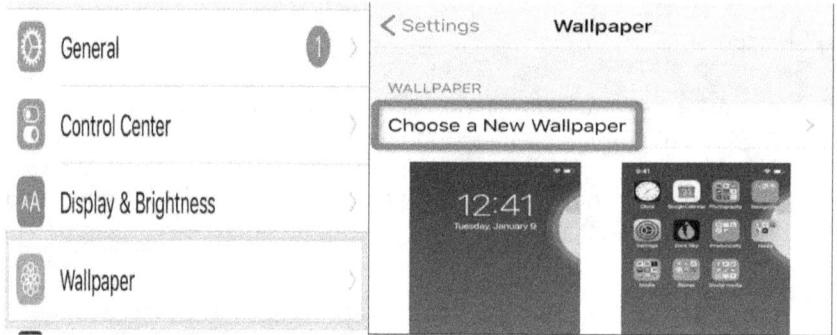

b) Photos Library:

- Select a photo from your library, adjusting the scale and alignment to fit your preference.

- Consider the clarity, color balance, and subject of the photo for optimal aesthetics.

c) Online Resources:

- Discover a plethora of wallpaper options available on websites, forums, and apps, catering to diverse tastes and interests.

2. Setting Wallpaper for Lock Screen, Home Screen, or Both

- After selecting a wallpaper, decide whether to set it for the Lock Screen, Home Screen, or both.

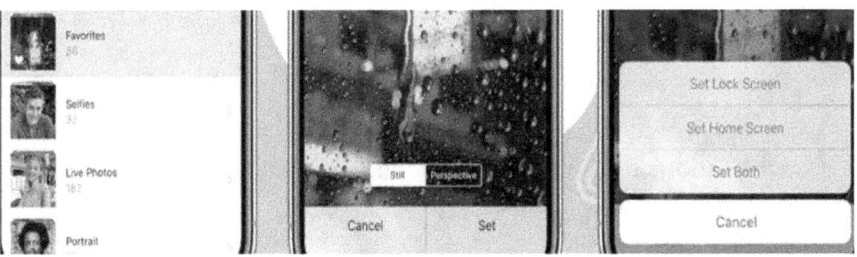

- Preview how the wallpaper aligns with app icons, time, date, and other elements on both screens.

3. Live and Dynamic Wallpapers

a) Live Wallpapers:

- Interact with your wallpaper by pressing and holding on the Lock Screen to animate it.

- Note that Live Wallpapers only animate on the Lock Screen and appear as stills on the Home Screen.

b) Dynamic Wallpapers:

- Enjoy a subtle animation and shifting colors throughout the day with Dynamic Wallpapers.

- Consider the impact on battery life as dynamic elements can consume more power.

4. Creating Your Own Wallpaper

a) Photography:

- Capture high-quality photos with your iPhone 15 camera and edit them using the Photos app or third-party editing apps.

- Experiment with composition, lighting, and subject matter to create visually appealing wallpapers.

b) Digital Art Apps:

- Explore digital art apps like Procreate or Adobe Fresco to design custom wallpapers.

- Experiment with textures, layers, and colors to create a piece that resonates with your style.

5. Considerations for Wallpaper Selection

a) Visibility:

- Ensure that your chosen wallpaper does not obscure app icons, text, and interface elements.

- Opt for images with balanced contrast and color schemes for better visibility.

b) Mood and Personal Expression:

- Consider changing wallpapers seasonally, during holidays, or to match your mood or life events.

6. Parallax Effect and Perspective Zoom

- Decide whether to enable or disable Perspective Zoom when setting a wallpaper to add a parallax effect.

- Experiment with this feature to enhance the three-dimensional feel of your Home Screen and Lock Screen.

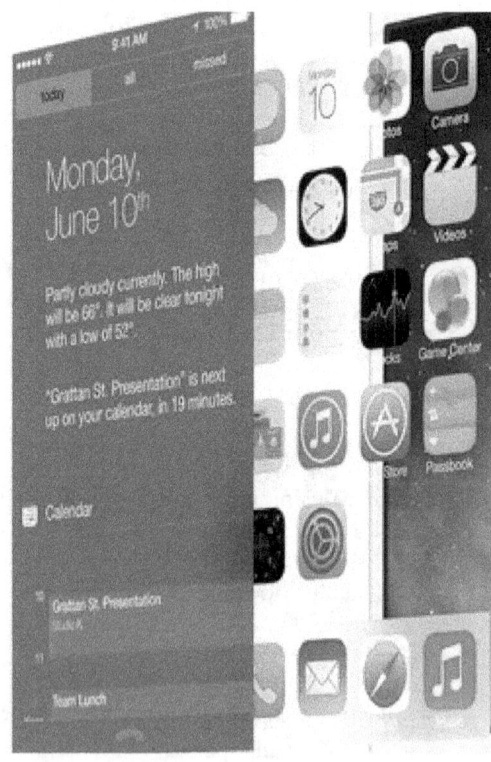

7.2 Organizing Apps

1. Arranging Apps on the Home Screen

a) Moving Apps:

- Touch and hold an app icon until it jiggles. Drag it to a new location or to the edges to move it to a different Home Screen page.

b) Creating Folders:

- Drag an app onto another app to create a folder. Rename the folder by tapping on the title.

2. App Library: A Categorized Overview

- Swipe to the far right of your Home Screens to access the App Library.

- Apps are automatically categorized, offering an organized overview and easy access through the search bar.

3. Creating Custom App Icons

a) Shortcuts App:

- Use the Shortcuts app to create custom app icons and personalize your Home Screen's appearance.

b) Adding to Home Screen:

- Once a custom icon is created, add it to your Home Screen and arrange it as per your liking.

4. Utilizing Folders Wisely

a) Categorization:

- Organize similar apps into folders such as Social, Productivity, Entertainment, etc.

5. Smart Stacks and Widgets

a) Adding Widgets:

- Touch and hold an empty space on the Home Screen to add widgets that offer quick functionalities.

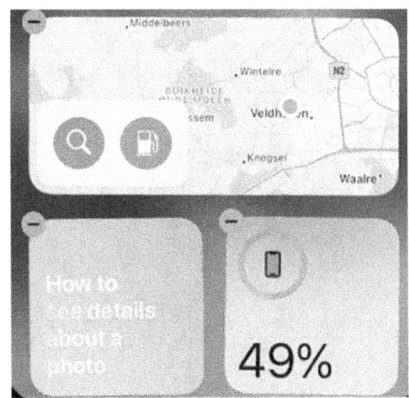

b) Smart Stacks:

- Create stacks of widgets that you can swipe through, and let iOS automatically showcase the most relevant widget based on time and usage.

6. Hiding and Unhiding Home Screen Pages

- Press and hold an empty space on the Home Screen, then tap on the page dots to edit pages.

- Select or deselect pages to hide or unhide them, streamlining your visual space.

7. Deleting and Offloading Unused Apps

a) Deleting Apps:

- Tap and hold an app icon, then select "Delete App" to remove it and its data from your device.

b) Offloading Apps:

- Under Settings > General > [Device] Storage, enable "Enable Offload Unused Apps" to allow iOS to remove unused apps but retain their data.

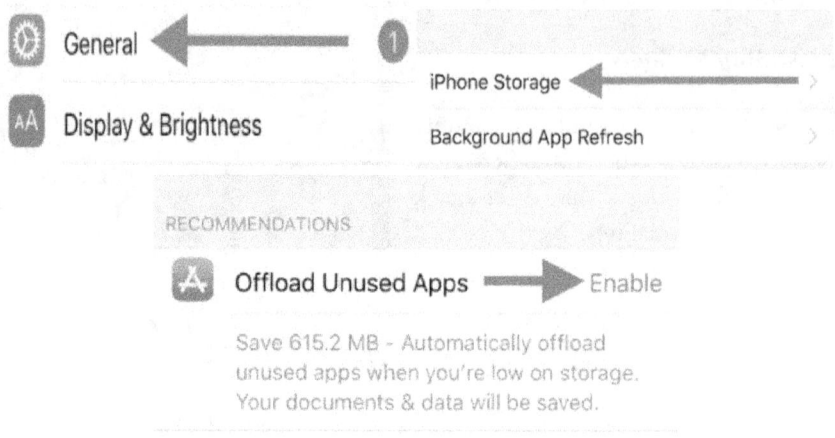

8. Organizing Apps in the Dock

- Place up to four apps or folders in the Dock for easy access from any Home Screen page.

- Consider organizing your most-used apps or a mix of folders and apps in the Dock.

7.3 Adjusting Sounds and Haptics

1. Managing Ringtones and Alert Tones

a) Selecting Ringtones:

- Navigate to Settings > Sounds & Haptics > Ringtone.

- Browse through the list of available ringtones, or tap "Tone Store" to purchase new ones.

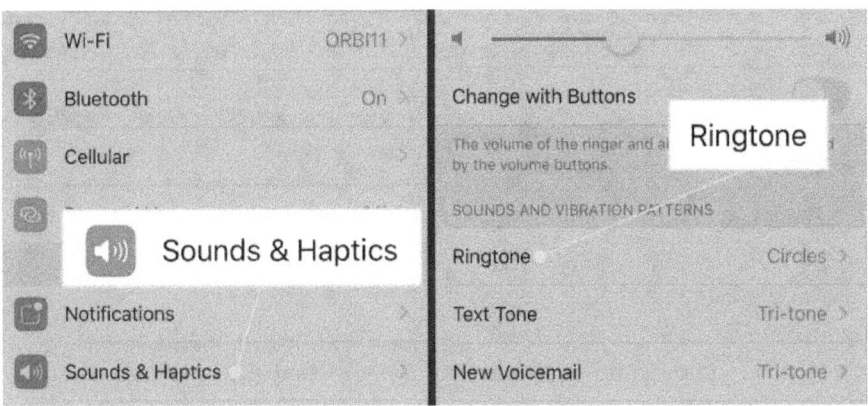

b) Text Tones and Alert Tones:

- Similarly, adjust text tones, voicemail, email, and other alerts.

- Consider assigning unique tones for different contacts or apps to identify them audibly.

2. Adjusting Volume and Vibration Patterns

a) Volume Controls:

- Manage the volume for media, ringtones, and alerts using the side buttons or through Settings > Sounds & Haptics.

- Enable "Change with Buttons" to adjust ringtone and alert volume using the volume buttons.

b) Vibration Patterns:

- Customize vibration patterns for different alerts and contacts under Settings > Sounds & Haptics.

- Create your own vibration pattern by tapping out a rhythm under "Vibration".

3. Enhancing Audio Experience

a) EQ Settings:

- Go to Settings > Music > EQ to adjust the equalizer settings for your audio playback.

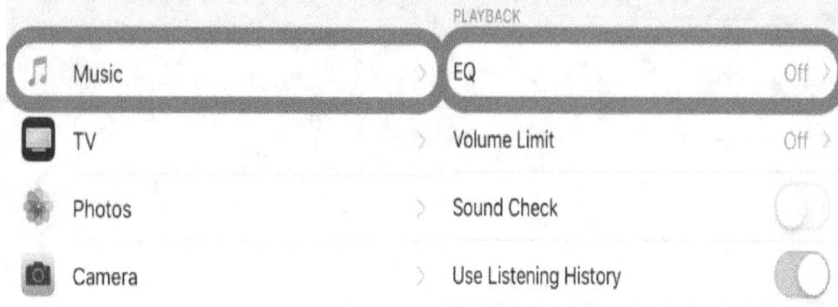

- Experiment with different presets to find the one that suits your music taste and headphone type.

b) Spatial Audio and Dolby Atmos:

- Enable Spatial Audio and Dolby Atmos for a surround sound experience in supported apps and content.

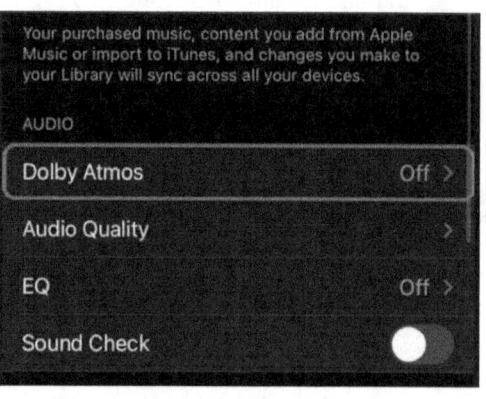

- Adjust the settings under Settings > Music > Dolby Atmos & Spatial Audio.

4. Modifying Haptic Feedback

a) System Haptics:

- Navigate to Settings > Sounds & Haptics to enable or disable System Haptics.

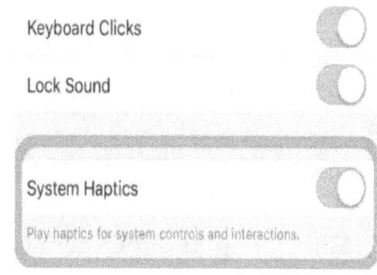

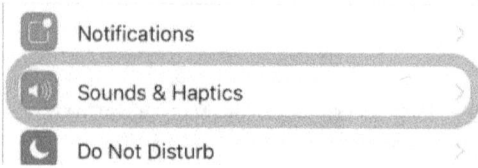

b) Haptic Touch:

- Customize the touch duration and intensity for Haptic Touch under Settings > Accessibility > Touch > Haptic Touch.

5. Managing Keyboard Clicks and Lock Sounds

- Toggle keyboard click sounds and lock sounds on or off under Settings > Sounds & Haptics.

- These adjustments contribute to a quieter or more tactile interaction with your device based on preference.

6. Optimizing Hearing Settings

a) Sound Recognition:

- Enable Sound Recognition under Settings > Accessibility > Hearing to let your iPhone listen for specific sounds and alert you.

b) Audio Accommodations:

- Adjust audio settings for balanced sound output and enhanced audio experience under Settings > Accessibility > Audio/Visual.

7. Setting Up Emergency Alerts

- Manage your emergency alert preferences under Settings > Notifications > Government Alerts.

- Enable or disable AMBER alerts, Emergency Alerts, and Public Safety Alerts based on your preferences.

Chapter 8: Accessibility Features

1. Vision

a) VoiceOver:

- Discover VoiceOver, a gesture-based screen reader that lets you enjoy the fun and functionality of your iPhone even if you can't see the screen.

- Learn to navigate, adjust settings, and use apps with the assistance of VoiceOver.

b) Magnifier and Zoom:

- Explore Magnifier and Zoom functions designed to enlarge text and images, making them easier to see for visually impaired users.

- Understand customization options for adjusting zoom levels, filters, and contrast.

c) Display and Text Size Adjustments:

- Learn how to modify display settings, including text size, boldness, and contrast, to improve visibility.

2. Hearing

a) Hearing Aids and Sound Recognition:

- Familiarize yourself with seamless connectivity options for Made for iPhone Hearing Aids and sound adjustments.

- Explore Sound Recognition, a feature that notifies you when the iPhone detects specific sounds in your environment.

b) Live Listen and Mono Audio:

- Learn about the Live Listen feature that turns your iPhone into a remote microphone for your hearing aid.

3. Mobility

a) Touch Accommodations and AssistiveTouch:

- Explore Touch Accommodations, which adjust the way your iPhone responds to touches.

- Discover AssistiveTouch, allowing you to control your iPhone using on-screen touch gestures, customized actions, and adaptive switches.

b) Switch Control and Voice Control:

- Learn about Switch Control, which lets you interact with your iPhone using external switches and various accessories.

- Familiarize yourself with Voice Control, an advanced voice recognition system that allows you to navigate and perform tasks using voice commands.

4. Learning and Literacy

a) Guided Access and Safari Reader:

- Discover Guided Access, which limits your iPhone to a single app and allows you to control app features.

- Explore Safari Reader, which provides a distraction-free reading environment by simplifying webpage layouts.

b) Spoken Content and Predictive Text:

- Learn about Spoken Content, which reads out text on your screen and provides additional spoken cues.

5. General Accessibility Features

a) Accessibility Shortcut and Siri:

- Familiarize yourself with the Accessibility Shortcut, which provides quick access to frequently used accessibility features.

- Explore how Siri can be a helpful assistant for individuals with accessibility needs, answering queries, and performing tasks through voice commands.

b) Customization and Compatibility:

- Dive into the extensive customization options available for all accessibility features to suit individual needs.

8.1 Vision Accessibility

1. VoiceOver

a) Introduction to VoiceOver:

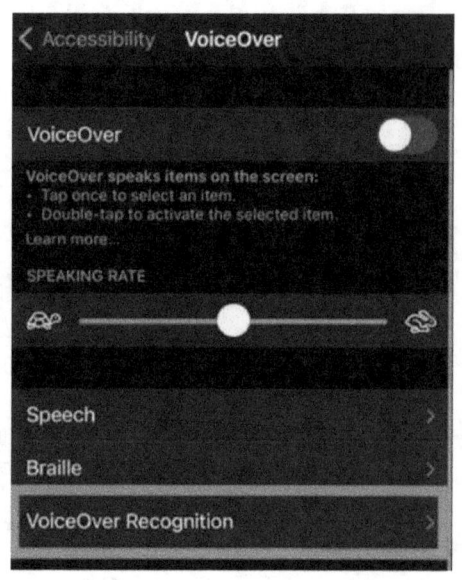

- Learn about VoiceOver, Apple's screen-reading technology, enabling users with visual impairments to interact with their devices.

- Explore the interactive nature, gestures, and voice commands that make navigation and interaction smooth.

b) Customizing VoiceOver:

- Delve into the customizable settings, adjusting the speaking rate, voice pitch, and verbosity.

- Discover Braille support, enabling seamless interaction with Braille displays.

2. Zoom and Magnifier

a) Utilizing Zoom:

- Get acquainted with Zoom, a powerful built-in magnifier that can enlarge content up to fifteen times the original size.

- Learn to adjust Zoom settings, such as zoom level, filters, and the Zoom Controller.

b) Magnifier App:

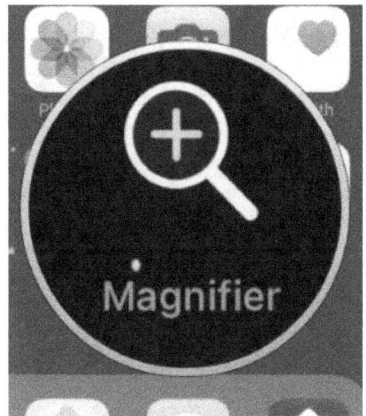

- Discover the dedicated Magnifier app, which turns your iPhone camera into a magnifying glass for real-world objects.

- Explore customization options including adjusting contrast, brightness, and applying color filters.

3. Display Adjustments

a) Text and Display Customization:

- Learn about modifying text size, boldness, and contrast for optimal visibility.

- Explore the different font options and discover how to leverage True Tone for ambient light adjustment.

b) Color Filters and Inversions:

- Understand how to apply and customize color filters for color vision deficiencies.

- Learn about Smart Invert and Classic Invert for reversing display colors.

4. Speak Screen and Speak Selection

a) Activating and Using Speak Screen:

- Discover how to make your iPhone read out all visible content with a simple swipe-down gesture.

- Explore the customization of voices, speaking rate, and highlight content as it's being read.

b) Leveraging Speak Selection:

- Learn about selecting text and having your iPhone read it back to you.

- Customize the Speak Selection settings for a personalized experience.

5. Braille Support and Voice Control

a) Braille Input and Output:

- Explore Braille input directly on the iPhone screen, enabling typing in Braille without a physical Braille keyboard.

- Discover the compatibility with various Braille displays and learn about Braille commands.

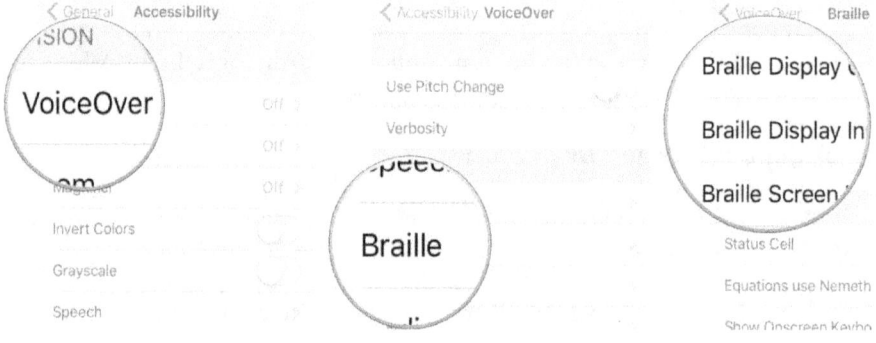

b) Voice Control for Visual Impairments:

- Understand how to use Voice Control as a user with visual impairments, leveraging voice commands for navigation and interaction.

- Customize Voice Control settings to suit individual needs and preferences.

6. Additional Accessibility Settings

a) Accessibility Shortcut:

- Learn about setting up and using the Accessibility Shortcut for quick access to your most-used accessibility features.

b) Compatibility with Third-Party Devices:

- Explore the range of third-party devices and accessories that can further enhance the visual accessibility of your iPhone.

- Learn about setting up and integrating these devices for a seamless user experience.

8.2 Hearing Accessibility

1. Hearing Devices Compatibility

a) Made for iPhone Hearing Aids:

- Discover the seamless integration and benefits of using Made for iPhone Hearing Aids.

- Learn how to pair, control, and adjust settings of your hearing aids directly from your device.

b) Sound Processor Support:

- Explore compatibility with cochlear implants and bone conduction sound processors.

- Understand the customization and control available for these sound processors through the iPhone.

2. Sound Recognition

a) Activating and Using Sound Recognition:

- Learn how to enable Sound Recognition, allowing your iPhone to listen for and identify specific sounds in the environment.

- Customize notifications and understand how this feature can assist in day-to-day awareness.

b) Sound Recognition in Practice:

- Discover real-world applications and benefits of using Sound Recognition.

- Explore tips and best practices for using this feature effectively.

3. Live Listen

a) Setting Up and Utilizing Live Listen:

- Understand the functionality and benefits of the Live Listen feature, which turns your iPhone into a remote microphone.

- Learn how to set up and use Live Listen with your hearing aids or AirPods for enhanced sound clarity.

b) Practical Scenarios for Live Listen:

- Explore various scenarios where Live Listen can be particularly beneficial, such as crowded environments or meetings.

- Gain insights into optimizing the use of Live Listen for different situations.

4. Mono Audio and Balance

a) Enabling Mono Audio:

- Discover Mono Audio, a feature that combines left and right audio channels for users with hearing loss in one ear.

- Learn how to activate Mono Audio and adjust the balance for personalized listening.

8.3 Mobility Accessibility

1. Touch Accommodations

a) Understanding Touch Accommodations:

- Learn about how Touch Accommodations adjust the way your iPhone responds to touch, making it more accessible.

- Discover how to enable and customize settings like Hold Duration and Ignore Repeat.

b) Using AssistiveTouch:

- Dive into AssistiveTouch, which lets users customize gestures and create touch screen shortcuts.

- Explore creating custom gestures, adjusting touch areas, and activating menus with AssistiveTouch.

2. Switch Control

a) Activating and Navigating with Switch Control:

- Understand how Switch Control allows users to navigate sequentially through onscreen items and perform specific actions.

- Discover how to set up switches and customize settings for scanning, timing, and navigation.

b) Creating Recipes and Custom Commands:

- Explore the creation of Recipes for custom gestures and actions.

- Learn how to use and manage multiple switch recipes for different tasks and apps.

3. Voice Control

a) Setting Up and Customizing Voice Control:

- Delve into Voice Control, allowing users to command their iPhone entirely with their voice.

- Learn about customization, creating custom commands, and refining voice recognition.

b) Practical Applications of Voice Control:

- Discover various scenarios where Voice Control can be highly beneficial.

- Learn tips and strategies for effectively using Voice Control in everyday situations.

4. Keyboard and Text Input

a) Onscreen and External Keyboard Options:

- Understand the various adaptations available for onscreen and external keyboard use.

- Learn about Sticky Keys, Slow Keys, and Key Repeating adjustments.

b) Dictation and Third-Party Keyboards:

- Explore the use of Dictation for text input and controlling the device.

- Discover compatible third-party keyboards offering additional accessibility features.

5. Accessibility Shortcut and Siri

a) Customizing Accessibility Shortcut:

- Learn how to set up and use the Accessibility Shortcut for quick access to your most-used accessibility features.

- Explore the customization of multiple features with a triple-click of the side button.

b) Utilizing Siri for Mobility:

- Understand how Siri can be a powerful tool for users with mobility impairments.

- Learn voice commands and explore the integration of Siri with other accessibility features.

6. Additional Customizations and Accessories

a) Customizing the Home Button and Gestures:

- Explore the various settings available for adjusting the click speed of the Home button.

- Learn about customizing system gestures to suit individual mobility needs.

b) Compatible Accessories for Enhanced Accessibility:

- Discover a range of third-party accessories and devices that can further enhance the iPhone's accessibility.

- Learn how to integrate these accessories effectively for an optimized user experience.

Chapter 9: Maintaining Your iPhone

1. Battery Health and Optimization

a) Monitoring Battery Health:

- Learn how to access the Battery Health feature and interpret the Maximum Capacity and Peak Performance Capability readings.

- Understand the significance of optimized battery charging and how to enable it.

b) Adopting Energy-Efficient Practices:

- Discover tips and habits to extend battery life, such as adjusting screen brightness, updating apps, and managing background app activities.

2. Regular Software Updates

a) Importance of Software Updates:

- Understand why keeping the iOS and apps up to date is crucial for performance, security, and accessing new features.

- Learn how to check for available updates and install them.

b) Preparing for Updates:

- Discover best practices for preparing your iPhone for an update, including backing up data and ensuring sufficient storage space.

- Explore troubleshooting steps in case of update issues.

3. Managing Storage Space

a) Monitoring and Managing Storage:

- Learn how to check your iPhone's available storage space and understand the categories consuming the most space.

- Discover how to manage storage by deleting unnecessary files, offloading unused apps, and utilizing iCloud storage.

b) Optimizing Photos and Messages Storage:

- Explore settings and features to optimize storage used by Photos and Messages apps, such as enabling iCloud Photos and managing message attachments.

4. Cleaning and Protecting the Exterior

a) Cleaning the Screen and Body:

- Understand the recommended methods and materials for cleaning the iPhone screen, camera lenses, and body to avoid damage.

- Learn about the importance of using microfiber cloths and avoiding abrasive materials.

b) Using Protective Accessories:

- Discover a variety of protective cases and screen protectors available for the iPhone 15.

- Learn how to choose the right accessories for your needs and lifestyle.

5. Security and Privacy Measures

a) Regularly Changing Passcodes and Passwords:

- Understand the significance of regularly updating passcodes and app passwords.

- Learn how to change passcodes and manage passwords securely using Apple's Keychain.

b) Managing App Permissions:

- Discover how to review and adjust app permissions to safeguard your privacy and data.

- Learn about the implications of granting apps access to location, contacts, camera, and other sensitive information.

6. Troubleshooting Common Issues

a) Restarting and Resetting:

- Learn the differences between restarting, force restarting, and resetting your iPhone.

- Discover when to use each method and how they can resolve various common issues.

b) Seeking Professional Assistance:

- Understand when it is necessary to seek help from Apple Support or authorized service providers.

- Learn about the warranty, AppleCare+, and the process of diagnosing and repairing issues.

9.1 Software Updates

What are Software Updates?

At their core, software updates are modifications made to software after its initial release. These changes can range from minor bug fixes and performance improvements to major feature rollouts and critical security patches.

There are two primary categories of software updates:

1. **Patches:** These are smaller updates targeted at fixing specific problems in the software, such as bugs, vulnerabilities, or performance issues. Patches are generally quick to install and are often essential for maintaining the security and stability of an application.

2. **Version Updates:** These can be minor or major and involve introducing new features, overhauling existing ones, or redesigning the user interface. Major version updates often come with a change in the software's version number, like going from version 1.0 to 2.0.

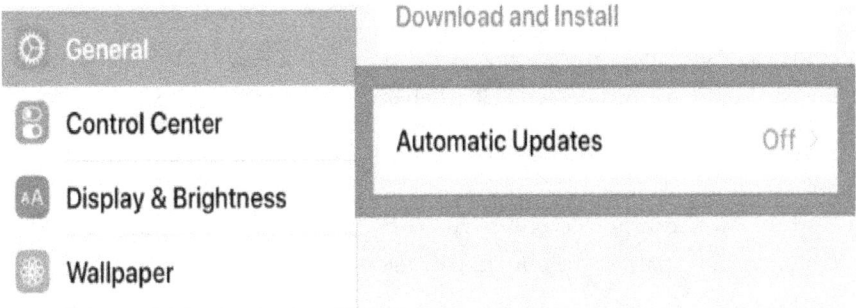

Why are Software Updates Important?

1. Security

The most critical reason to update software is security. With cyber threats growing more sophisticated, software developers continually identify and address vulnerabilities in their applications.

2. New Features

Developers frequently introduce new tools, functions, and capabilities in their updates. These enhancements not only provide users with a richer experience but also help software stay competitive and relevant in its domain.

3. Performance

Over time, as more data is processed and stored, software may begin to lag or crash. Updates optimize the software's performance, ensuring smoother and faster operation.

4. Compatibility

With the continuous evolution of technology, newer devices, and operating systems get released. Software updates ensure that applications remain compatible with the latest technological changes.

Challenges with Software Updates

1. Disruption

Updates, especially major ones, can disrupt a user's workflow. This is especially true for businesses that rely heavily on specific software.

2. Bugs

New updates, ironically, can introduce new bugs even as they fix others. This is an inevitable part of the software development cycle.

3. Resistance to Change

Users often become accustomed to a certain layout or feature set. When these are changed or removed, it can cause dissatisfaction.

Best Practices for Updating Software

1. **Backup Data:** Always backup important data before installing a major update to prevent data loss in case of unforeseen complications.

2. **Read Release Notes:** These notes provide information on what has been changed, added, or removed, preparing users for what to expect.

3. **Stagger Updates:** For businesses, it's often wise to stagger updates. Update a few systems first to ensure there are no major issues before rolling out to the entire organization.

4. **Stay Informed:** Subscribe to software vendors' newsletters or alert systems to be notified of critical updates, especially security patches.

9.2 Storage Management

Understanding Storage Management

Storage management is the systematic process of optimizing, provisioning, and maintaining the storage resources in a computing environment. It encompasses everything from physical storage devices like hard drives and SSDs to logical storage constructs like file systems, databases, and even cloud storage solutions.

The Importance of Storage Management

1. Cost Efficiency

Well-managed storage helps in maximizing the use of available space, reducing the need for unnecessary hardware purchases.

2. Data Accessibility

Effective storage management ensures that data is available and retrievable whenever needed, leading to better workflow efficiency.

3. Data Protection

A structured storage system makes it easier to implement backup and recovery solutions, safeguarding critical data against loss or corruption.

4. Performance Optimization

Organized storage systems often result in faster data retrieval times, boosting the overall system performance.

Challenges in Storage Management

1. Data Growth

With the exponential increase in data generation, scaling storage solutions without disruption becomes a challenge.

2. Data Redundancy

Managing duplicate or outdated data can consume unnecessary storage resources and lead to confusion.

3. Security Concerns

Ensuring that sensitive data is both accessible and protected from unauthorized access is a delicate balancing act.

Techniques for Effective Storage Management

1. Hierarchical Storage Management (HSM)

HSM solutions move data between high-performance and low-cost storage media based on its usage and importance. Frequently accessed data remains on faster storage, while less crucial data gets moved to cheaper, slower storage.

2. Data Deduplication

This technique identifies and eliminates redundant data, ensuring only one unique instance of the data exists on the storage.

3. Thin Provisioning

Instead of allocating physical storage space in advance, thin provisioning allocates virtual space as needed, optimizing storage utilization.

4. Storage Virtualization

It abstracts the physical storage from the logical storage, pooling multiple storage devices and allowing them to be managed as a single entity.

5. Automated Backup and Recovery

Implementing automated backup solutions ensures data protection. Regular recovery drills ensure that data can be restored effectively when needed.

6. Cloud Storage Solutions

Using cloud storage can offload some of the storage management responsibilities while providing scalability and remote access benefits.

Future Trends in Storage Management

1. **Software-Defined Storage (SDS):** Decoupling the storage software from its hardware gives businesses greater flexibility and scalability.

2. **Machine Learning and AI in Storage:** Machine learning algorithms can predict storage needs and automate many storage management tasks, making the processes more efficient.

9.3 Battery Health and Charging

The Science of Batteries

Before diving into maintenance and charging practices, it's essential to understand the fundamental operation of batteries. Most modern electronics, especially smartphones and laptops, use lithium-ion (Li-ion) or lithium-polymer (LiPo) batteries. These batteries offer high energy densities, allowing our devices to run longer between charges.

Indicators of Battery Health

1. Capacity

Measured in milliamp-hours (mAh), capacity indicates the amount of energy a battery can hold. As batteries age, their capacity diminishes, leading to shorter time between charges.

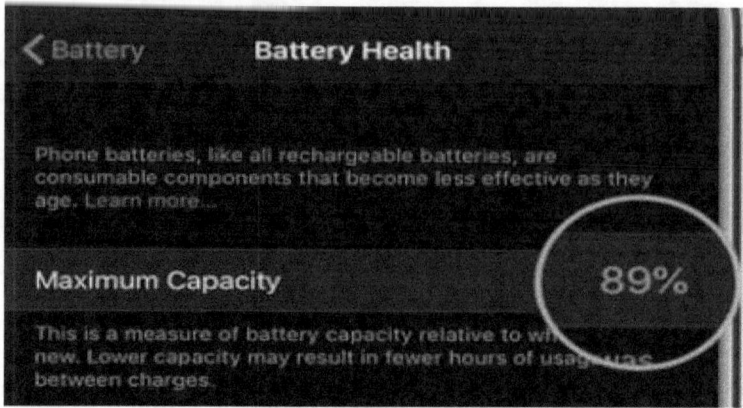

Factors Affecting Battery Health

1. Temperature

Exposing batteries to extreme temperatures, especially heat, can accelerate degradation.

2. Deep Discharges

Consistently draining your battery to very low levels can negatively impact its longevity.

3. Overcharging

While modern devices have mechanisms to prevent true overcharging, keeping a battery at 100% for extended periods can be detrimental.

Tips for Maintaining Battery Health

1. Optimal Charging Range

It's often recommended to keep lithium-based batteries between 20% and 80%. This range promotes battery longevity.

2. Avoid Heat

Don't leave devices in hot environments, like a car's dashboard in the summer. Heat is a battery's enemy.

3. Use Official Chargers

While aftermarket chargers can be cheaper, they may not adhere to the device's charging specifications, potentially harming the battery.

4. Calibration

Every few months, it's beneficial to let the battery drain and then charge it fully. This process can recalibrate the battery's software estimation for more accurate reading.

5. Storage

If you're not using a device for an extended period, store it with a charge level of around 50% to maintain battery health.

The Future of Battery Technology and Charging

1. Solid-State Batteries

Promising higher capacities, longer lifespans, and faster charging times, solid-state batteries could revolutionize our devices.

2. Wireless Charging Evolution

With the increasing prevalence of wireless charging, future advancements might offer faster and more efficient wireless power transfers.

3. AI-Powered Charging

With machine learning and AI, devices can adapt charging patterns based on user habits, maximizing battery lifespan.

Chapter 10: Security and Privacy

1. Fundamental Security Measures

a) Setting Up Face ID

- Learn the technology behind Apple's facial and fingerprint recognition and the steps to set them up.

- Understand the benefits, limitations, and best practices for using these biometric authentications.

b) Using Passwords:

- Discover the importance of strong passwords and how they encrypt your device.

- Get tips on creating and managing robust passcodes.

2. Data Protection and Encryption

a) iOS Encryption:

- Understand the fundamentals of data encryption on your iPhone.

- Learn about the encryption process, from device startup to file system protection.

b) iCloud Security:

- Explore the protective layers ensuring your iCloud data is secure, from two-factor authentication to end-to-end encryption.

- Learn how to enable and manage iCloud security settings.

3. App Privacy and Permissions

a) App Tracking Transparency:

- Understand Apple's stance on app tracking and the measures in place to give users control.

- Learn how to manage which apps can track your activity across other companies' apps and websites.

b) Reviewing and Adjusting App Permissions:

- Learn how to access and modify permissions given to apps, ensuring they only access essential data.

- Understand the implications of granting apps specific permissions, such as location access or microphone usage.

4. Safari and Web Privacy

a) Intelligent Tracking Prevention:

- Dive into how Safari prevents advertisers from tracking your online activities without compromising website functionality.

- Learn how to adjust Safari settings for optimal privacy.

b) Managing Cookies and Web Data:

- Understand the role of cookies in web browsing and the privacy implications.

- Discover how to view, manage, and delete cookies and other website data.

5. Privacy Preserving Features

a) Differential Privacy:

- Learn about the concept of differential privacy, which allows Apple to gather user data without identifying individual users.

- Understand its application in services like Maps, News, and more.

b) Minimizing Data Collection:

- Understand Apple's data minimization principle, which ensures only essential data is collected and stored.

- Learn about instances where this principle is applied, like in the Maps app or Siri requests.

6. Secure Communication with Messages and FaceTime

a) End-to-End Encryption:

- Dive into the end-to-end encryption mechanism that ensures only the sender and recipient can access the content of Messages and FaceTime calls.

- Learn about the benefits and underlying technology.

b) Managing Message and FaceTime Privacy:

- Discover settings to optimize privacy during communications, from filtering unknown senders to managing FaceTime caller ID.

7. Finding and Erasing Lost iPhones

a) Activating Find My iPhone:

- Learn how to set up and use the Find My iPhone feature.

- Understand its utility in locating a misplaced device and the technology behind its accurate tracking.

b) Remote Erase and Activation Lock:

- Discover how to erase your device data remotely if it's lost or stolen.

- Understand the Activation Lock mechanism that prevents anyone else from using your iPhone without your Apple ID.

10.1 Setting Up Face ID

1. Introduction to Biometrics on iPhone

a) Face ID:

- Discover the advanced technology behind Face ID: from infrared cameras to neural networks.

2. Setting Up Face ID

a) Enrolling Your Face:

- Navigate to 'Settings' > 'Face ID & Passcode'.

- Follow the on-screen instructions, positioning your face within the frame and moving it as directed.

- Understand the process: the iPhone will capture two scans of your face to complete the setup.

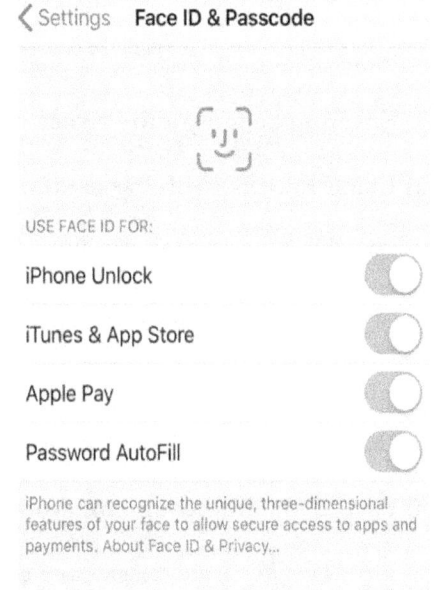

‹ Settings **Face ID & Passcode**

USE FACE ID FOR:

iPhone Unlock

iTunes & App Store

Apple Pay

Password AutoFill

iPhone can recognize the unique, three-dimensional features of your face to allow secure access to apps and payments. About Face ID & Privacy...

Set Up an Alternate Appearance

b) Alternate Appearance:

- Learn how to add an alternate appearance – handy for those times when your facial features might significantly change, such as with heavy makeup or facial hair alterations.

4. Using Face ID

a) Unlocking Your Device:

- For Face ID: Raise or tap to wake your device and glance at it.

b) Authenticating Payments and App Store Purchases:

- With Apple Pay, quickly double-click the side button for Face ID

- For App Store purchases, authenticate using the facial or fingerprint scan when prompted.

c) App Authentication:

- Recognize how third-party apps use Face ID as secure authentication methods, eliminating the need for passwords.

5. Ensuring Security and Privacy

a) Using Face ID with Passcodes:

- Understand that for added security, your iPhone will sometimes request your passcode even if Face ID is enabled, such as after a restart or multiple unsuccessful attempts.

6. Troubleshooting Common Issues

a) Face ID Isn't Recognizing Me:

- Tips to ensure clear vision: check for obstructions like sunglasses or masks.

- Reset Face ID and set it up again.

7. Opting Out of Biometrics

a) Disabling Face ID :

- Navigate to 'Settings' > 'Face ID & Passcode' and select 'Turn Off'.

b) Privacy Considerations:

- Understand why some users opt for passcode-only security and the trade-offs involved.

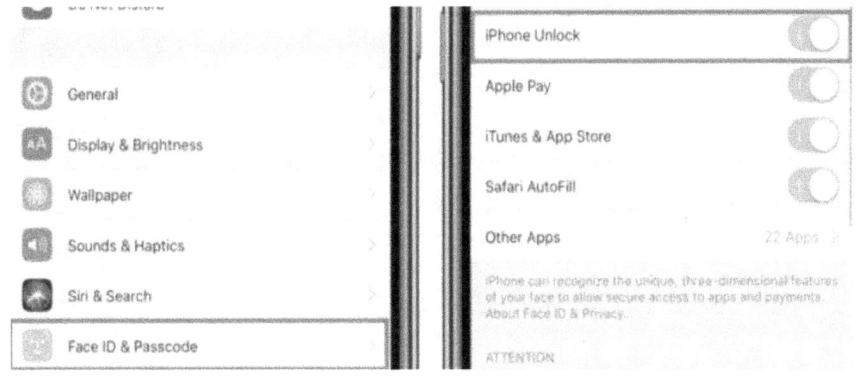

10.2 Privacy Settings

1. Navigating to Privacy Settings

a) Accessing the Privacy Menu:

- Open the 'Settings' app and tap on 'Privacy' to view a list of all the features and apps that request access to your personal data.

b) General Overview:

- Familiarize yourself with the layout of the Privacy settings and the different categories available.

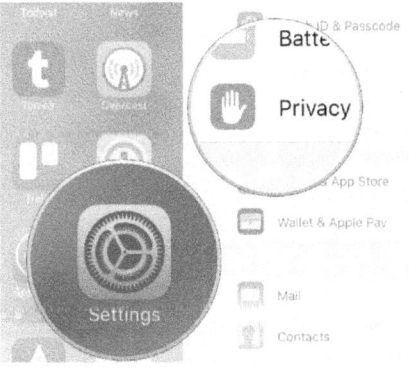

2. Location Services

a) Managing Location Access:

- Learn how to turn Location Services on or off.

- Understand the different types of location access you can grant to apps: 'Never', 'Ask Next Time', 'While Using the App', or 'Always'.

b) System Services and Significant Locations:

- Dive into system services that utilize your location, such as 'Find My iPhone', 'Share My Location', and 'Emergency Calls & SOS'.

- Discover 'Significant Locations', a feature where your iPhone learns places significant to you – and how to manage or clear this data.

3. Tracking and Advertisements

a) Managing App Tracking:

- Understand Apple's App Tracking Transparency feature.

- Learn how to allow or disallow apps from requesting to track your activity across other companies' apps and websites.

b) Personalized Ads:

- Dive into the world of Apple's advertising platform and how it respects user privacy.

4. Control Over App Permissions

a) Reviewing App Access:

- Examine which apps have access to specific data like contacts, calendars, photos, and more.

- Learn how to grant or revoke access to ensure only trustworthy apps can access sensitive data.

b) App-Specific Permissions:

- Understand more about permissions related to Bluetooth, microphone, speech recognition, and other sensors.

- Explore best practices for managing these permissions to enhance privacy.

5. Analytics & Improvements

a) Sharing with Apple:

- Learn about the data Apple may collect to improve its products and services.

- Discover how to toggle off sharing iPhone analytics, iCloud analytics, and more.

b) Sharing with App Developers:

- Understand the implications of sharing crash data and usage information with app developers.

- Decide whether to share or withhold this data based on your comfort level.

6. Apple ID Management

a) Access and Manage Data:

- Learn how to view the data associated with your Apple ID and request a copy, correct inaccuracies, or deactivate your account.

b) Two-Factor Authentication:

- Dive into the added security layer that is Two-Factor Authentication (2FA).

- Discover how to set up 2FA for your Apple ID to further safeguard your account.

7. Additional Privacy Tips

a) Regularly Reviewing Permissions:

- Understand the importance of routinely revisiting your privacy settings to manage app permissions, especially after downloading new apps.

b) Staying Updated:

- Emphasize the significance of keeping your iOS updated to benefit from the latest security patches and privacy enhancements.

10.3 Apple Pay and Wallet

1. Introduction to Apple Pay and Wallet

a) What is Apple Pay?

- Discover Apple's secure, contactless payment system that uses your iPhone, Apple Watch, iPad, or Mac.

b) The Wallet App:

- Introduction to the app that manages credit, debit, and store cards, as well as tickets, boarding passes, and more.

Face ID

2. Setting Up Apple Pay

a) Adding a Card:

- Navigate to the Wallet app and tap the '+' sign or go to 'Settings' > 'Wallet & Apple Pay' > 'Add Card'.

- Follow the on-screen instructions, which may require you to scan your card or enter details manually.

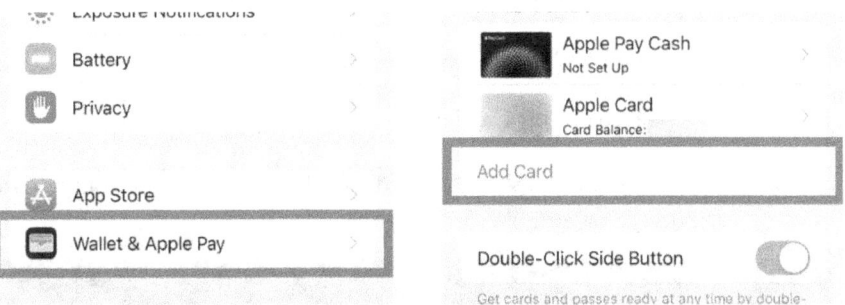

b) Authenticating with Your Bank:

- Depending on your bank, you might receive a verification code via text, email, or a phone call. Enter this code to authenticate.

3. Using Apple Pay

a) In Stores:

- For iPhone: Double-click the side button and authenticate using Face ID, then hold your phone near the terminal.

- For Apple Watch: Double-click the side button and hold your watch close to the terminal.

b) In Apps and Online:

- Look for the "Buy with Apple Pay" or "Apple Pay" button during checkout.

- Authenticate the purchase using Face ID, or your passcode.

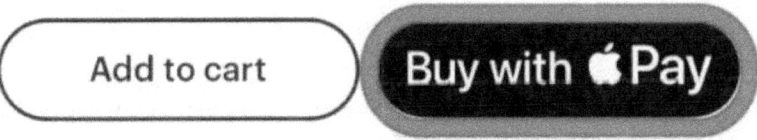

4. Managing Cards in Wallet

a) Setting a Default Card:

- Learn how to select a default card to prioritize during transactions.

b) Updating or Removing Cards:

- Navigate to 'Settings' > 'Wallet & Apple Pay'. Here, you can update card details or remove cards entirely.

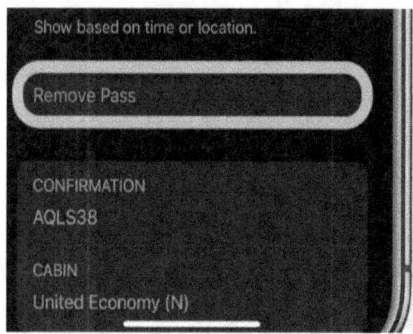
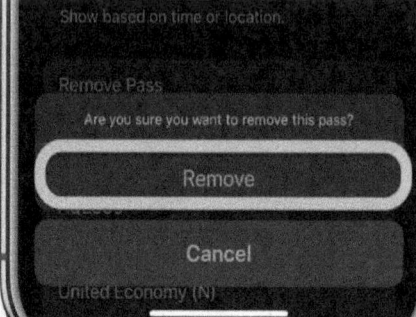

5. Using the Wallet App

a) Adding Passes and Tickets:

- From movie tickets to boarding passes, learn how to add items to Wallet either manually or via supported apps.

b) Using Rewards Cards and Coupons:

- Discover how to integrate store loyalty cards or digital coupons, ensuring you always have them on hand.

6. Security and Privacy

a) Secure Element and Device Account Number:

- Understand the Secure Element chip's role in transaction security.

- Learn about the Device Account Number, a unique, encrypted number generated for each card, ensuring card details are never shared with merchants.

b) Transaction Verification:

- Face ID or your passcode are required for every transaction, adding an extra layer of security.

c) Monitoring Transactions:

- Check your recent transactions in the Wallet app, providing an easy way to monitor your spending.

7. Troubleshooting and Tips

a) Failed Transactions:

- Common reasons for failure and steps to resolve them.

b) Lost iPhone or Apple Watch:

- Using 'Find My', you can put your device in Lost Mode or erase it entirely, ensuring your financial details are safe.

c) Tips for Faster and Efficient Use:

- From ensuring your device's NFC is functioning to regularly updating your card details, gather pro tips for smoother transactions.

Chapter 11: Siri and Voice Commands

1. Introduction to Siri

a) The Genesis of Siri:

- A brief history of Siri's development and integration into the Apple ecosystem.

b) How Siri Works:

- Understand the artificial intelligence, machine learning, and voice recognition technologies underpinning Siri.

2. Setting Up Siri

a) Activating Siri:

- Navigate to 'Settings' > 'Siri & Search' and enable 'Listen for "Hey Siri"'.

- Go through the brief setup to train Siri to recognize your voice.

b) Language and Voice Customization:

- Choose from a variety of voices and select your language preference.

3. Interacting with Siri

a) Basic Commands:

- **"Hey Siri, what's the weather like today?"**

- **"Hey Siri, set an alarm for 7 am."**

- Get acquainted with a list of fundamental commands to get started.

b) Complex Queries:

- Dive deeper with commands like, "Hey Siri, find emails from John from last week."

- Learn to chain commands for multitasking.

4. Siri Shortcuts

a) Creating Custom Commands:

- Discover how to set up custom phrases that trigger specific actions, like "Hey Siri, I'm going home" to get directions to your house, send a text to a family member, and play your favorite playlist.

b) Using the Shortcuts App:

- Explore the integrated Shortcuts app to create complex automations, combining multiple tasks into one voice command.

5. Siri in Different Applications

a) Music and Entertainment:

- "Hey Siri, play the latest album by Taylor Swift."

- Control media playback and discover content.

b) Messaging and Communication:

- "Hey Siri, text Mom I'll be there in 10 minutes."

- Learn how to send, read, and reply to messages hands-free.

c) Productivity:

- "Hey Siri, remind me to call the bank at 3 pm."

- Set reminders, schedule meetings, and manage your tasks.

6. Enhancing Privacy

a) Siri and Data Handling:

- Understand how Apple handles voice data and the steps taken to ensure user privacy.

b) Managing Siri History:

- Learn how to delete Siri interactions and voice recordings.

7. Troubleshooting Common Issues

a) Siri Not Responding:

- Tips for ensuring your microphone is clear and that Siri is set up correctly.

b) Improving Voice Recognition:

- Train Siri to better understand your voice and accent.

8. Expanding Siri's Capabilities

a) Third-Party App Integration:

- "Hey Siri, order a pizza from Domino's."

- Discover how to use Siri with compatible third-party apps to streamline various actions.

b) HomeKit and Siri:

- "Hey Siri, turn off the living room lights."

- Explore the integration of Siri with Apple's HomeKit for smart home control.

11.1 Setting Up Siri

1. Activating Siri on Your iPhone

a) Enabling Siri:

- Navigate to 'Settings'.

- Scroll down and tap on 'Siri & Search'.

- Toggle on 'Listen for "Hey Siri"'.

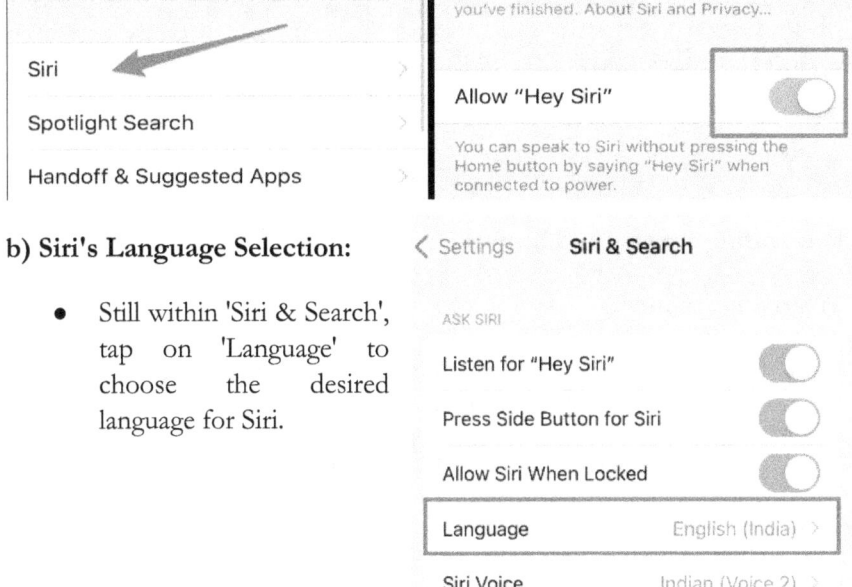

b) Siri's Language Selection:

- Still within 'Siri & Search', tap on 'Language' to choose the desired language for Siri.

2. Personalizing Siri's Voice

Apple provides a selection of voices for Siri, allowing users to choose the one that resonates best with them.

- In 'Siri & Search', tap on 'Siri Voice'.

- Listen to the available voice options and select your preferred voice.

3. Train Siri to Recognize Your Voice

When you enable "Hey Siri," you'll be prompted to train Siri to recognize your voice. This ensures that Siri responds primarily to you.

- Follow the on-screen instructions, which will ask you to speak a few phrases such as "Hey Siri, how's the weather today?"

- This process helps Siri identify the nuances in your voice, reducing false activations.

4. Activate Siri with a Button Press

While "Hey Siri" is convenient, there are times press and hold the side button until the Siri waveform appears.

5. Ensuring Privacy and Security

a) Siri Suggestions:

- Within 'Siri & Search', you can choose whether Siri makes suggestions on the lock screen, in search, or when sharing.

- Toggle these options on or off based on your preference.

b) Personal Requests:

- This allows Siri to access your messages, reminders, and more when your iPhone is locked. Decide if you want this feature on for added convenience or off for increased privacy.

6. Integrating Siri with Other Apps

a) Siri App Support:

- Still within 'Siri & Search', scroll to find a list of apps.

- Click on each app to see and customize how Siri interacts with it. You can choose to allow or disallow Siri to search within certain apps.

7. Siri Feedback

Decide how you want Siri to provide feedback:

- Navigate to 'Settings' > 'Accessibility'.

- Scroll down and tap 'Siri'.

- Here, you can choose if you want Siri to always respond with voice feedback or only when you say "Hey Siri" or use the side/Home button.

8. Advanced Customization with Siri Shortcuts

For users looking to delve deeper:

- Explore the 'Shortcuts' app, which integrates closely with Siri.

- Create custom commands for Siri, from sending pre-drafted messages to executing a series of tasks with a single command.

11.2 Using Siri for Everyday Tasks

1. Messaging and Communication

a) Sending Texts:

- "Hey Siri, text [Contact Name] 'I'm on my way.'"

- Siri will draft the message, and you can confirm to send it.

b) Reading Out Texts:

- "Hey Siri, read my latest message from [Contact Name]."

- Siri will read out the message, ensuring hands-free communication.

2. Organizing Your Day

a) Setting Alarms and Reminders:

- "Hey Siri, set an alarm for 6:30 am tomorrow."

- "Hey Siri, remind me to call the dentist at 3 pm."

b) Calendar Events:

- "Hey Siri, schedule a meeting with [Contact Name] next Friday at 2 pm."

3. Information On-the-Go

a) Weather Updates:

- "Hey Siri, what's the weather like today?"

- Stay prepared by checking the forecast for your location or any other city.

b) Quick Conversions and Calculations:

- "Hey Siri, how many ounces are in a liter?"

- "Hey Siri, what's 18% of 250?"

4. Entertainment and Media

a) Music Commands:

- "Hey Siri, play my Workout playlist."

- "Hey Siri, skip to the next song."

5. Navigation and Travel

a) Directions:

- "Hey Siri, how do I get to the nearest gas station?"

- Siri integrates with Apple Maps to provide real-time directions.

b) Travel Information:

- "Hey Siri, what's the status of flight AA101?"

- Stay updated on your travel plans.

6. Food and Dining

a) Finding Nearby Restaurants:

- "Hey Siri, show me the top-rated Italian restaurants near me."

b) Setting Dining Reminders:

- "Hey Siri, remind me to make a reservation at [Restaurant Name] for Saturday evening."

7. Shopping and To-Do Lists

a) Creating Lists:

- "Hey Siri, add 'buy milk' to my grocery list."

- Manage your tasks efficiently, ensuring nothing gets missed.

b) Checking Items:

- "Hey Siri, what's left on my grocery list?"

8. Quick Information and Fact-Checking

a) Quick Facts:

- "Hey Siri, who wrote 'Pride and Prejudice'?"

- "Hey Siri, when did World War II end?"

b) Currency Rates:

- "Hey Siri, what's the current exchange rate for USD to EUR?"

9. Integration with Smart Home Devices

If you have smart devices connected via Apple's HomeKit:

a) Controlling Lights:

- "Hey Siri, turn off the living room lights."

b) Adjusting Thermostat:

- "Hey Siri, set the temperature to 72 degrees."

10. Using Siri for Relaxation

a) Meditation and Sleep Timers:

- "Hey Siri, play the sound of rain for 20 minutes."
- Use Siri to help you relax or set sleep timers for peaceful nights.

Chapter 12: Troubleshooting Common Issues

1. iPhone Doesn't Turn On

a) Hard Reset:

- Quickly press and release the Volume Up button, then the Volume Down button, then press and hold the Side button until the Apple logo appears.

b) Charge the Battery:

- **Sometimes the battery is fully drained.** Connect your iPhone to a charger and wait for a few minutes.

2. iPhone Screen is Frozen

a) Restart Your iPhone:

- Turning it off and then back on can resolve many minor glitches.

3. Apps Crash or Become Unresponsive

a) Close and Reopen the App:

- Swipe up from the bottom of the screen and pause to open the App Switcher. Swipe the app's preview off the screen to close it.

b) Update the App:

- Go to the App Store and check "Updates" to ensure the app is updated to the latest version.

c) Reinstall the App:

- Delete and then reinstall the app from the App Store.

4. iPhone is Overheating

a) Remove the Case:

- Some cases might cause the iPhone to retain more heat.

b) Keep Away from Direct Sunlight:

- Extreme environmental conditions can affect the iPhone's performance.

5. No Sound or Distorted Sound

a) Check the Mute Switch:

- Ensure the mute switch on the side isn't activated.

b) Clean the Speaker:

- Use a soft brush to gently clean any debris from the speaker grills.

c) Adjust Volume Settings:

- Ensure the volume is turned up, and no headphones are connected.

6. WiFi Connectivity Issues

a) Toggle WiFi On and Off:

- Go to 'Settings' > 'Wi-Fi' and toggle it off, wait a few seconds, and turn it back on.

b) Restart Your Router:

- Occasionally, the issue may be with the router itself.

c) Forget and Rejoin Network:

- In 'Wi-Fi' settings, tap the "i" icon next to the network, select "Forget This Network," and then rejoin.

7. iPhone is Running Slow

a) Update iOS:

- Ensure you're running the latest version by going to 'Settings' > 'General' > 'Software Update'.

b) Clear Unnecessary Files:

- Use 'Settings' > 'General' > 'iPhone Storage' to review and delete unused apps or large media files.

c) Restart Your iPhone:

- This can help refresh its memory.

8. Battery Drains Fast

a) Check Battery Usage:

- Under 'Settings' > 'Battery', review which apps are consuming the most power.

b) Adjust Background App Refresh:

- Go to 'Settings' > 'General' > 'Background App Refresh' and turn off apps you don't need to update in the background.

c) Update iOS:

- Some updates might include optimizations to improve battery life.

9. Face ID Isn't Working

a) Ensure Cleanliness:

- Wipe the camera or home button to ensure no dirt or moisture affects recognition.

b) Reset Face ID

- Go to 'Settings' > 'Face ID & Passcode' to reset and reconfigure.

12.1 Restarting and Resetting

1. Restarting Your iPhone

To address minor glitches such as unresponsive apps or a frozen screen, restarting your iPhone can be effective.

- Briefly press and release the Volume Up button.

- Briefly press and release the Volume Down button.

- Hold the Side button until you see the Apple logo, then let go.

2. Soft Reset

A soft reset clears all active processes and temporary data without erasing your content.

- Press and Hold Side Button and Volume Button: Press and hold either the volume up or volume down button and the side button simultaneously until two sliding buttons appear.

- Slide to Power Off: Drag the slider that says "slide to power off" to the right. Your iPhone will turn off.

- Restart the iPhone: After the device turns off, press and hold the side button again until you see the Apple logo.

3. Hard Reset (Force Restart)

Use this approach if your phone is completely unresponsive.

- For iPhones without a Home Button: Press and release Volume Up, then Volume Down, followed by holding the Side button until the Apple logo shows.

- For iPhones with a Home Button: Simultaneously hold the Home and Top (or Side) buttons until the Apple logo appears.

4. Reset All Settings

This resets all settings to their original state but keeps your data intact.

- Navigate to 'Settings' > 'General' > 'Reset' > 'Reset All Settings' and enter your passcode if prompted.

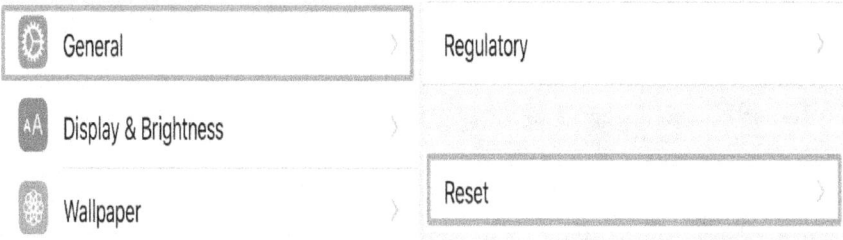

5. Erase All Content and Settings (Factory Reset)

For a complete data wipe, ideal when transferring ownership of your iPhone:

- Back up your device first.
- Proceed to 'Settings' > 'General' > 'Reset' > 'Erase All Content and Settings' and confirm your choice.

Erase All Content and Settings

6. Reset Network Settings

To resolve network issues by resetting all network-related settings:

- Go to 'Settings' > 'General' > 'Reset' > 'Reset Network Settings'.

Reset Network Settings

7. Reset Keyboard Dictionary

To remove custom words and reset your keyboard dictionary:

- Go to 'Settings' > 'General' > 'Reset' > 'Reset Keyboard Dictionary'.

Reset Keyboard Dictionary

8. Reset Home Screen Layout

To revert your home screen to the default app arrangement:

- Head to 'Settings' > 'General' > 'Reset' > 'Reset Home Screen Layout'.

Reset Home Screen Layout

9. Reset Location & Privacy

To reset all your location services and privacy settings:

- Visit 'Settings' > 'General' > 'Reset' > 'Reset Location & Privacy'.

Reset Location & Privacy

12.2 Seeking Apple Support

1. Apple Support Website

The first stop for many users, Apple's official support website, is a comprehensive resource. Here, you can:

- **Browse Popular Topics:** These articles cover the most common issues and their solutions.

- **Search for Specific Issues:** Input keywords or error codes into the search bar for targeted advice.

2. Apple Support App

Available on the App Store, the Apple Support app is a convenient way to:

- **Diagnose Issues:** The app can run diagnostic tests to identify problems.

- **Chat with an Advisor:** Real-time text-based support from Apple experts.

- **Schedule Calls or Appointments:** If you need more in-depth assistance or want to visit an Apple Store.

3. Genius Bar Appointments

Found at every Apple Store, the Genius Bar offers face-to-face technical support. Remember to:

- **Book in Advance:** Appointments can be scheduled through the Apple Support app or website.

- **Backup Beforehand:** If there's a chance your device might need to be reset or replaced, backup all important data.

4. Apple Phone Support

To speak directly with an Apple representative:

- **Find the Support Number:** Apple's website lists phone numbers by region.

- **Prepare Your Device:** Have your iPhone's model and serial number ready, as well as a description of the issue.

5. Apple Community Forums

For issues that aren't necessarily technical glitches:

- **Search Existing Threads:** Someone might have faced a similar challenge.

- **Post a New Question:** Detail your problem and wait for community members or Apple experts to provide solutions.

6. AppleCare and AppleCare+

If you've purchased an AppleCare plan:

- **Extended Support:** AppleCare extends the regular warranty and provides additional phone or in-person support.

- **Accidental Damage:** AppleCare+ includes limited coverage for accidental damages, with a service fee per incident.

7. Service and Repair

For hardware-related issues or damages:

- **Check Your Warranty:** Visit Apple's warranty status page by inputting your serial number.

- **Service Options:** Depending on the issue and warranty status, Apple might offer mail-in service, carry-in service, or even an express replacement.

8. Training and Workshops

If you're looking to maximize your iPhone use:

- **Today at Apple:** These in-store sessions range from basic introductions to advanced software use.

Chapter 13: Closing Thoughts

As we draw this guide to a close, it's important to pause and reflect on the journey we've taken together. Exploring the intricacies of the iPhone, understanding its vast functionalities, and adapting to its innovative features, we've delved deep into the heart of a device that is more than just a piece of technology; it's an integral part of our daily lives.

1. Evolution of Technology

One can't help but marvel at how far we've come. From the first iPhone, which was groundbreaking in its own right, to the current iPhone 15, Apple has consistently pushed the boundaries of what a smartphone can be. This guide, while detailed for the current model, also serves as a testament to the relentless march of innovation.

2. More than Just a Device

Our smartphones are no longer just tools; they're extensions of ourselves. They capture our memories, connect us to our loved ones, assist in our work, and entertain us. They have a footprint in nearly every aspect of our lives.

3. The Importance of Continuous Learning

While this guide is comprehensive, the world of technology is ever-evolving. New updates, apps, and features will continuously emerge. Stay curious. Keep learning. Embrace changes, and remember that with every new feature or app, there's an opportunity to enhance your user experience.

4. Safety, Security, and Responsibility

As we've discussed, with great power comes great responsibility. The iPhone provides us with incredible capabilities, but it's crucial to use it safely, responsibly, and ethically.

5. The Community Aspect

Owning an iPhone isn't just about the device; it's about being a part of a global community. Sharing tips, helping out fellow users, or simply discussing favorite features—these communal aspects enrich the overall experience.

6. Gratitude and Acknowledgment

Finally, it's essential to acknowledge the myriad of developers, designers, engineers, and thinkers behind this device. Their vision, expertise, and dedication have given us this remarkable piece of technology that fits right into our palms.

13.1 Embracing Technology

1. The Pace of Progress

Just a few decades ago, the idea of holding a device with the power of a supercomputer in our pockets seemed like a distant fantasy. Today, it's our reality. This swift transformation is a testament to humanity's relentless drive for progress. Embracing technology means appreciating its pace while ensuring we don't feel overwhelmed.

2. Digital Integration, Not Replacement

Technology should augment our lives, not replace the fundamental aspects of our human experience. While virtual meetings can connect global teams, they can't replace the warmth of a handshake or the joy of a shared laugh. As we integrate technology into our routines, it's crucial to strike a balance, ensuring we use tools to enhance real-life experiences, not overshadow them.

3. Continuous Learning

The landscape of technology is ever-shifting, with new tools and platforms emerging regularly. Embracing this realm means fostering a spirit of continuous learning. Whether it's mastering a new app, understanding a software update, or diving into the world of augmented reality, staying curious will ensure you remain not just relevant but also engaged.

4. Digital Well-being

While technology offers unparalleled convenience, it can also lead to digital fatigue. Embracing technology means setting boundaries. Schedule screen-free time, engage in digital detox weekends, or simply practice mindfulness exercises to ensure that while you're connected to the world, you're also connected to yourself.

5. Ethical Use and Digital Citizenship

As digital citizens, we bear the responsibility of using technology ethically. This means respecting digital privacy, not spreading misinformation, and understanding the implications of our online actions. Embracing technology means recognizing its power and using it with respect and integrity.

6. Nurturing Human Connections

In a world where 'liking' a post is a click away, it's essential to nurture genuine human connections. Use technology as a bridge, not a barrier. Send a heartfelt message, video call a distant friend, or use apps to engage in shared hobbies. Let technology be a conduit for genuine human interaction.

7. Preparing for the Future

The horizon of technology is brimming with promises of artificial intelligence, virtual realities, and interconnected smart cities. While we can't predict every twist and turn, we can prepare by staying informed, adaptable, and open-minded.

13.2 Resources and Additional Help

1. Official Apple Support

Apple's official support platform is your first point of contact for any issues, queries, or information related to your iPhone.

- **Website:** https://support.apple.com

- **Apple Support App:** A dedicated app available on the App Store that offers personalized recommendations, organized product information, and more.

- **Apple Community Forums:** Connect with other Apple users, share issues, and find solutions collaboratively.

2. Online Tutorials and Courses

If you're looking to expand your knowledge or master specific features:

- **Udemy:** An online learning platform with courses on a variety of iPhone topics, from photography to productivity.

- **Lynda (now LinkedIn Learning):** Features professional video tutorials on Apple products and software.

3. Blogs and Websites

Numerous tech bloggers and websites offer in-depth reviews, tutorials, tips, and tricks for iPhone users:

- **MacRumors:** For the latest news and rumors related to Apple products.

- **iMore:** Comprehensive guides, reviews, and how-to articles on everything Apple.

4. YouTube Channels

Visual learners might benefit from video tutorials and reviews:

- **EverythingApplePro:** Regular updates on the latest Apple products, reviews, and hacks.

- **Apple Insider:** Offers in-depth reviews, news, and tutorials.

- **iJustine:** A tech enthusiast who covers a broad range of Apple products with a fun and engaging approach.

5. Podcasts

For those who enjoy on-the-go learning:

- **MacBreak Weekly (MBW):** A weekly roundtable discussion about all things Apple.

- **The CultCast:** Covers the latest Apple news in an entertaining manner.

6. Third-Party Apps

There are many apps designed to help you optimize and troubleshoot your iPhone experience:

- **iMazing:** Offers a comprehensive iOS device manager that goes beyond iTunes' capabilities.

- **PhoneClean:** An app to optimize iPhone performance and clear unnecessary files.

7. Local Workshops

Check for local workshops or classes in community centers, libraries, or tech stores. Apple Stores worldwide also offer "Today at Apple" sessions where you can learn various aspects of your device.

Conclusion

From the moment you unboxed your iPhone 15 to the deeper exploration of its myriad features, capabilities, and applications, this guide has accompanied you every step of the way. But as with all journeys, there is an eventual culmination, a point where we reflect on the trails traveled and anticipate the paths ahead.

The iPhone, beyond its intricate circuitry and sleek design, represents a beacon of human innovation and creativity. It's not just a tool or an accessory, but a testament to our shared desire for connection, exploration, and expression. With every tap, swipe, and voice command, we're not just navigating a device – we're navigating our own narratives in this digital age.

While this guide aimed to provide a comprehensive overview, technology, in its ever-evolving glory, is boundless. New apps will emerge, software updates will refine experiences, and fresh challenges will arise. But with the foundation of knowledge you've acquired, you're not just prepared; you're empowered.

Remember, technology is a double-edged sword. While it has the power to simplify, amplify, and beautify aspects of our lives, it's crucial to wield it with intentionality, ensuring it complements rather than consumes our existence. Cherish face-to-face conversations, savor moments without the compulsion to capture them, and occasionally, look up from the screen to soak in the beauty of the tangible world.

Finally, this book, like your iPhone, is but a tool. The real magic lies in how you use it, the memories you create, the connections you foster, and the horizons you dare to explore. As you continue your digital voyage with the iPhone 15 and beyond, may curiosity be your compass and purpose your anchor.

Thank you for allowing this guide to be a part of your journey. Here's to countless discoveries, joys, and innovations that await you. Embrace the digital era with an open heart and a discerning mind, and remember – the best is yet to be. **Stay connected, and until next time, happy exploring!**

www.ingramcontent.com/pod-product-compliance
Lightning Source LLC
Chambersburg PA
CBHW072207290526
45794CB00004B/1680